MILLIONAIRES
& BILLIONAIRES

MILLIONAIRES
& BILLIONAIRES

At Last... Billion Dollar Strategies for Creating Wealth & Success

DARREN J STEPHENS & SPIKE HUMER

DISCLAIMER

A note on currencies used in this book: currencies used are those of the home country of each person profiled. Unless otherwise noted, dollars are US, and pounds are UK.

All the information, techniques, skills and concepts contained within this publication are of the nature of general comment only and are not in any way recommended as individual advice. The intent is to offer a variety of information to provide a wider range of choices now and in the future, recognising that we all have widely diverse circumstances and viewpoints. Should any reader choose to make use of the information contained herein, this is their decision, and the contributors (and their companies), authors and publishers do not assume any responsibilities whatsoever under any condition or circumstances. It is recommended that the reader obtain their own independent advice.

First Edition 2010

National Library of Australia
Cataloguing-in-Publication entry:

Millionaires & Billionaires Secrets Revealed / Darren Stephens & Spike Humer.
Other Authors/Contributors: Humer, Spike.

1st ed.
ISBN: 9781921630477 (pbk.)

Finance, Personal.
Investments.
Success in business.
Millionaires--Australia--Anecdotes.

332.02401

Published by Global Publishing Group
PO Box 517 Mt Evelyn, Victoria, 3796, Australia
Email: info@TheGlobalPublishingGroup.com

For Further information about orders:
Phone: +61 3 9736 1156 or Fax: +61 3 8648 6871

We dedicate this book to all the people who dare to dream and who have the courage, persistence and commitment to take action to achieve those dreams.

Darren Stephens & Spike Humer

Acknowledgements

It has been an honour and privilege to write this book. As with any major project, there are a number of very special people who contributed to making this book happen. So, we'd like to take this opportunity to say "THANK YOU".

A special Thank You to the 9 Awesome Entrepreneurs/Leaders featured in this book. Your willingness to share your secrets is a priceless gift. It has been an honour and a tremendous privilege to work and learn from every one of you and we're sure that thousands of people's lives will be influenced by the stories and insights that you've shared.

We'd like to thank the many other mentors, models, guides, colleagues and friends who have taught us, supported us and inspired us along the way. Most are giants in their fields, many are geniuses in their own way, and all are gifts in our lives.

In business people like Jay Abraham, Chet Holmes, Tom Hopkins, Keith Cunningham, Stephen Covey, Brian Tracy, Matt and Amanda Clarkson, Daryl and Andrew Grant, Loral Langemeier, Marshall Thurber, Bret Thomson, Greg Cassar, Mike Rhodes, Richard and Veronica Tan, Bernardo Moya, Koichiro Shimizu, Tony Giannopoulos, Pat Mesiti, Rich Schefren, Brian Johnson, Stephen Pierce and Dr. Tom Hill have been important sources for our success.

In personal growth, people such as Dr. Richard Bandler, John and Kathleen LaValle, Tony Robbins, Jim Rohn, John Overdurf and Julie Silverthorn and Anthony de Mello helped light our path along the way.

In philosophy and spirituality, Dr. Wayne Dwyer, Sri Sai Kaleshwara Swami, The Dalai Lama, Eckhart Tolle, Carlos Castaneda, Marianne Williamson, Ram Dass, Ken Wilber and Miguel Ruiz have served as guides along the path of living and growing.

In health, wellness and relationships, Jackie Tallentyre, Dr. John Gray, Andrew Weil, Dr. Daniel Amen, Dr. Mehmet C. Oz, Robert A. Johnson, Jon Kabat-Zinn, and Leo Buscaglia have been important teachers, speakers and authors who have helped us grow.

Most significantly, we'd like to thank Colin and Carlee Frankel, Fletcher and Carole Searle, John Gearon, Michael Dean, Luke Raisbeck, Narelle and Jason Urbanowicz, Darren Tagg, Kevin Stephens, Jeni Stephens, Norm Herbert, Lisa and Shane Bell, Larry Lindt, Mel Kerr, Brian Gerhart, Fred Martin, Paul Dwyer, Manny Goldman, Brendon Bruchard, Debra Kezer, Maria Davis, Vanessa Pedzwater, and "Big Bill" McKee for their support, contribution, advice and counsel throughout our lives and careers.

Next, a huge thanks to our students and joint venture platinum partners for their ongoing support and trust in allowing us to guide them to future success.

A huge Thank You to our publisher, Global Publishing Group and to their awesome team; Jo Munro, Kelly Mehlert and Sonia Vasey. And to Joel Fulton and the team at Dennis Jones & Associates for your dedication and commitment to the book's success.

A special Thank You to our parents and our beautiful children.

And, finally, we thank our beautiful wives, Jackie and Michele. They're a constant and tremendous source of insight, wisdom and support to us.

EXTRA BONUSES!!

We can't give you everything you need to know about becoming Rich and Successful in one small book.

So we've created lots of extra special goodies, just for you. You'll find lots of money making Bonuses that will help fast track your success. There are checklists and tools to help you grow your business and success. There's even downloadable videos.

Go check out our resources and FREE success tools NOW at:

www.DarrenJStephens.com

www.SpikeHumer.com

Table of Contents

Introduction   1

Chapter 1   Richard Branson   3

Chapter 2   Bill Clinton   23

Chapter 3   Oprah Winfrey   43

Chapter 4   Pierre Omidyar   63

Chapter 5   Bill Gates   81

Chapter 6   Warren Buffett   105

Chapter 7   Tony Blair   137

Chapter 8   J.K. Rowling   155

Chapter 9   Larry Page   173

Authors' Final Word   188

About the Authors   190

Recommend Success Resources   195

Introduction

Some people come out of nowhere and build enormous success and fortune. They seem to be born as forces of nature and to rise like rockets well into the stratosphere, far above the rest of us, as though they were born under a different influence, able to see things and do things that most people can't. Enormously successful entrepreneurs, self-made people, super-successes and stars—call them what you will, people who elevate themselves to great wealth and success are rare, productive geniuses.

But, do such people really possess secrets or abilities that are unattainable by the average person? Are they born destined for success, whereas the average person is simply not that lucky? Or could we all achieve such success, if we just knew how?

You deal with dozens of Millionaires and billionaires every day. Just think about it.

This morning you awake to your Apple iPhone alarm(Steve Jobs, worth US$5.5 billion). Then, after packing your Louis Vuittion suitcase (Bernard Arnault, worth US$17.5 billion) you jumped onto your computer using Microsoft (Bill Gates worth 53 billion) you then Googled (Larry Page, worth US$17.5 billion) your flight details on the way out the door. In the taxi to the airport you caught up on the daily news reading The Australian newspaper (Rupert Murdoch, worth US$6.3 billion).

So with a billionaire around every corner, it begs the question: what do they have that most people don't?

The people who achieve great success certainly haven't done it by accident. Their achievements don't come easily and they aren't accomplished on autopilot. In fact, it is entrepreneurship, above all, that displays effort and deliberate thought. So, in fact, success is something that is available to anyone who is willing to put forth the effort.

So, what are the keys to success and how can you earn some of that wealth, too? If anyone who puts their mind to it can do it, how is it done, and why have we not already achieved it? The truth is, there is a difference between successes and average people. Average people have not yet succeeded beyond a certain point! But that doesn't mean that it can't be done. That's the reason for this book.

We will be taking a closer look at nine of the world's great success stories. These stories can be observed as blueprints for how to succeed. We can all learn their secrets. And then it will be time to go out and start building some wealth of your own.

Many of these so-called "secrets" are really surprisingly simple. Anyone can learn them. Look at what distinguishes these people and then apply those lessons. Here are their stories...

Cheers

Darren & Spike

Richard Branson

"A business has to be involving, it has to be fun, and it has to exercise your creative instincts."

MILLIONAIRES & BILLIONAIRES
SECRETS REVEALED!

Brief Overview

Sir Richard Branson

Born:	18th July, 1950, in London, UK
Business:	Virgin Group of companies
Industry:	Airlines, Communications, Finance, Retail
Income:	Net worth £2.6 billion US $3.9 billion
Lives:	London & Necker Island
Family:	Wife, Joan, and 2 children, Holly and Sam
Charities:	The Elders, International Rescue Corps, Prisoners Abroad, various others
Status:	Billionaire

Profile

We will kick off our look at larger-than-life lives with the man who epitomises the term: Richard Branson. The bad boy of self-made men is a colourful figure who seems to be just as at home on television and in magazines as he is in his office. If his face wasn't recognisable around the world, the beach-boy hair, toothy grin and deep smile lines might give a person the impression of no one more distinctive than a middle-aged outdoorsy type. But, as we all know, there is a great deal more to his story than that.

> "Branson thinks big. He dares to think things that no one else takes seriously."

Branson is a wildly successful entrepreneur with an incredible number of companies under the Virgin name. He is an unashamed self-promoter, being a rare entrepreneur who is as publicly visible as his recognisable red trademark; the Virgin company name. Richard Branson is also an old-fashioned adventurer, having set records and suffered many near-fatal mishaps by sea and air. Branson impresses one as a modern-day buccaneer, a man who screams through life at breakneck speed.

Branson thinks big. He dares to think things that no one else takes seriously, and he runs his business like a maverick pilot, flying by the seat of his pants. He has taken big risks his whole life and succeeded spectacularly.

Background

Richard Charles Nicholas Branson was born on July 18th, 1950 in London. His father, Edward James Branson, was a barrister and his mother, Eve, was a flight attendant. Branson was the first born of four children. Early on, he attended Scaitcliffe School. From the first, Branson had a very difficult time in school, due to the fact that he was attempting to deal with the problem of dyslexia. He nearly failed out of Scaitcliffe.

> "He actually attempted his first business venture at the age of 9."

Even at this tender age, however, he showed an aptitude for business. He actually attempted his first business venture at the age of 9. Branson attempted to sell Christmas trees, but this first foray into commerce failed. Another early effort to sell birds also failed.

When Branson was 13, he began attending Stowe School, in Buckinghamshire, England.

He continued with his academic struggle while boarding at Stowe. Struggle is, in fact, an understatement. He agonised over lessons, having to memorise word-for-word in order to recite in public. He was embarrassed over his abilities and had a terrible time with the standardised tests. His talents, while in school, were in sports. Branson excelled in sports, particularly in swimming. His affinity for water would play out later in his life. In the meantime, however, sports were the only bright spot in an otherwise grim educational experience. He could think outside the confines of academia, however.

He had identified a need. He noticed that, while young people were becoming increasingly aware and active, there was no consolidated "voice" for his generation. No one was really speaking to young people and no one was really speaking for them.

Branson was looking at the world around him, and he had a great talent for reading people, even if he could not read the written page without difficulty. He was seeing the changing attitudes around him in the youth movements of the late 60s.

> "I predict that you will either go to prison or become a millionaire."

Working with a friend, Branson put together *Student* when he was only 16 years old. He decided to put together a successful venture from the start by thinking big. This paper was aimed at the students of multiple schools, tying together a local population. He wanted to make it much bigger than a typical student paper by selling advertising to major corporations, and printing articles by famous people. The paper was produced out of his friend's parents basement, and the first issue was distributed for free, a total of 50,000 copies. The paper was paid for by advertising.

Branson dropped out of school, due to his difficulty there, in order to put his efforts into his newspaper. The final word on Branson, as a student, was provided by his headmaster at the time, who said, "I predict that you will either go to prison or become a millionaire." The headmaster's prescience was uncanny—Richard Branson has since done both.

The newspaper was a success, because Branson aimed high. He did not let the fact that he was a young dropout stop him from approaching the biggest names he could. Branson says that, "I remember when I was asking Vanessa Redgrave or James Baldwin for an interview and the fact that they took the time to respond meant an enormous amount to me. It inspired me. So it's extremely important to respond to people and to give them encouragement if you're a leader."

From the single venture of Branson's paper, further establishments grew and spread, like ripples on a pond. In 1970, when Branson was 20 years old, Branson saw another opportunity.

The Retail Price Maintenance Agreement was abolished by the British government. This agreement kept records from being sold at discount prices, but this would be possible after the regulation was ended. However, record stores did not voluntarily discount their prices, and Branson took action.

He began a mail-order discount record company advertised through his own paper. His readership, as Branson well knew, was hungry for music and willing to pay. The record company took off and Branson expanded by adding to his staff and taking a space above a shoe store to distribute his records.

His new employees wanted to think of a company name that would reflect the new business and be more dynamic than "Student". Names like "Slipped Disc" were considered and discarded before one associate suggested Virgin, because they were all untried and untested in business. And the first Virgin company was born.

The young Richard attempted a daredevil move in order to sell the discount vinyl and to avoid taxes. Record makers would sell "cut-out" discs that had been returned unsold from retailers, so-called due to the fact that these records would by marked by cutting off a corner, or cutting a notch or hole into the spine of the jacket. Branson travelled to the continent to purchase crates of these cut-outs. He would then return to London with the records in the back of his van to be sold at his bargain prices to retailers. This way Branson avoided paying a purchase tax and saved about £5,000.

After several trips, Branson attracted the attention of the Customs and Excise office. He was arrested and he spent a night in jail. The fines were steep, as Richard needed £15,000 immediately in order to be released and would need to eventually pay a total of £45,000 to keep the incident off of his criminal record.

Branson's intrepid mother came to his rescue at this point, mortgaging her home to get Richard out of jail. Richard redoubled his efforts with Virgin to make the money to pay the fines. In a strange way, prison fuelled the growth of the future Virgin Megastores. Branson was arrested in 1971.

He opened his first record shop in Oxford Street in 1972, two years after beginning the mail-order business. The shops made money through retail concerns, and also exported records. Branson says in his autobiography that "avoiding prison was the most persuasive incentive I've ever had. Since there was limited growth left in the mail-order business, we concentrated on expanding the record shops. The next two years were a crash course in how to manage cash. From being a completely relaxed company running on petty cash from the biscuit tin and a series of unpaid IOU notes, we became obsessively focused. We used every penny of the cash generated from the shops towards opening up another shop, which in turn was another pound towards paying off my Customs and Excise debt. Eventually I was able to pay everything and relieve Mum of the bail she had put up."

Branson went on to open many other companies that form the Virgin Group. He purchased the nightclub Heaven in 1979. This was a gay nightclub near Charing Cross in London. In 1980, Virgin Records went international.

Branson continued to expand his influence in the entertainment industry with Virgin Vision, which later became Virgin Communications, which is a distribution company that sends films to television and radio broadcasting.

On the personal front, Branson has been married twice. He married Kristen Tomassi in 1972, at the age of 22. They were divorced four years later.

He has been married to his second wife, Joan, since 1977. In 1979, Branson suffered the biggest tragedy of his life. The couple's

> "Branson owns over 300 separate companies under the Virgin aegis."

first daughter, Clare Sarah, was born three months prematurely, and died a few days later.

Another year and a half later, their daughter Holly was born. She is now a doctor. The couple also have a son, Sam.

Today, Branson owns over 300 separate companies under the Virgin aegis. The net worth of his empire can only be estimated but, at last count, by some calculations, was worth £2.6 billion. That figure is far below some calculations, partly due to the recent economic downturn. It is also due in part to the fact that such figures are always in flux and estimates vary. In any case, the fortune is huge.

Wealth Accumulation

Branson actually credits his dyslexia for some of his business success, as much as it also caused his educational failures. Since he could not read and study business reports any more than he could school papers, he cultivated an intuitive sense of people and of business. His creative approach has put an indelible stamp on his corporate style.

Whatever his intuition told him, the record company, although struggling, was ultimately successful.

When musician Mike Oldfield met Branson, he was unsigned, and apparently unsignable. Branson, however, with his characteristic disregard for risk, simply decided to form a record label in order to publish this release.

With the money from his mail-order business, Branson built a studio in Oxfordshire. It was here that he oversaw the recording of his first vinyl album. Mike Oldfield recorded *Tubular Bells* and Branson began distribution of this album in 1973.

Thus was born Virgin Records. Oldfield's *Tubular Bells* rose to the top of the charts and the top of the best-selling records. This, of course, was just the beginning of Virgin Records.

Virgin rose to success by signing controversial and cutting-edge bands. They signed the Sex Pistols and later signed groups from Genesis to Culture Club.

Richard Branson was in touch with his generation and had already begun a strategy of operating a business successfully as an underdog. This is now as much a hallmark of his business model as his high-profile image.

With Virgin Records, Branson's early success was assured, and his image as an extraordinary entrepreneur was already solidified. Richard Branson had made a name for himself by the time he was 20 years old. His meteoric rise, and his fame, has not flagged since. He has spent more of his life in the spotlight than out of it.

In 1984, Virgin took another turn, unexpected and, in the opinion of many, doomed to fail. Not that such opinions have ever stopped Branson. Virgin Atlantic Airways was launched out of a simple (or simple-sounding) wish to live to the fullest and to overcome big challenges.

Branson's foray from the entertainment world into the realm of transportation might seem nonsensical from the outside, but to Branson it made sense. He is a man who quite simply makes things happen.

> "...never again to put himself in the power of bankers."

"My interest in life comes from setting myself huge, apparently unachievable challenges and trying to rise above them.... I felt that I had to attempt it."

Attempt it he did, and the rest is history. Virgin Atlantic was the nucleus of an empire. Branson expanded his transportation companies to include airlines worldwide. He eventually sold Virgin Records to keep the planes flying, much as it pained him.

This story illustrates the way in which Branson will do whatever it takes to succeed. Virgin Records had been the cornerstone of his empire and the original smash success. But, when it was struggling, Branson made the difficult decision to let it go.

Actually, Branson was pushed into this decision by bank managers to whom he was indebted for the airline. He claims that this taught him never again to put himself in the power of bankers.

The result of the painful personal and corporate decision was a one billion-dollar US deal with THORN EMI. After the 1992 sale, it is said that Branson cried over the loss of his label. He was not to stay out of the music business for long, however. He loves the business. He founded the Virgin Radio station the next year.

By 1996, V2, Branson's next label, was founded. He was back in his beloved music industry.

The continued success of Virgin Atlantic allowed Branson to further expand the Virgin trademark. He went into telecommunications, and expanded to hundreds of companies. These range from a brand of vodka to a stem cell bank.

Most of Branson's ventures are concentrated in the entertainment, transportation and communication industries. After launching his airline in 1983, Virgin expanded into an early satellite music station with Virgin Vision's "Music Box". Virgin Records expanded to the United States in 1984. By 1987, the Virgin Group, with some partners, founded British Satellite Broadcasting with five satellite channels in the United Kingdom.

Other production companies, games companies and travel companies were launched throughout the 1980s. During the 1990s, Virgin continued to expand with new entertainment companies. He also expanded his travel ventures with Virgin Trains. This decade also saw Branson's expansion into telecommunications, financial services, beverages like vodka and soft drinks, a rugby team, a cosmetics company, and a bridal store. He also launched Virgin. Net in 1996.

During the 2000s, Virgin went into the energy business, as a result of Branson's interest in alternative fuels. He expanded into a health bank, other media and cars. He is interested in running trains and cars with energy-efficient fuels, and runs a Formula One race car on this principle.

What started as a student newspaper is now a multi-billion pound media, transportation and lifestyle empire. Branson is one of the most recognisable entrepreneurs in the world.

In fact, the world might not be big enough for Sir Richard. He dared to begin the company Virgin Galactic. This company aims to do no less than carry paying passengers into space.

Ambition and risk are only part of the Branson style. He has preserved his entrepreneurial spirit through decades of doing business. His style comes from his understanding of and talent for reaching people.

Branson is closely involved with the management of only his record and airline companies. Typically, though, he is a very hands-off man when it comes to running a company. He famously enters into realms in which he has no expertise. He buys a company and sometimes retains the controlling interest. He is far from controlling, however.

Instead, he tends to look for the right person for the job and his acumen and judgment in this area is where his real expertise lies. Branson says that he finds someone who has a passion, interest, and talent for any particular company, and then instructs that person to run the company as if it were his or her own.

While he does not directly manage the operations of all of these companies, he is accessible. He writes (literally writes, since he does not use computers) monthly letters to his employees, keeping the tone chatty and informal. He also encourages all of his employees to come to him with concerns or ideas, which he then might decide to back up with his support. When he makes a decision of this kind, he really does back it up. Every employee of a company with Branson in an executive chair has his phone number and home address.

One of his employees, a flight attendant on Virgin Airlines, was planning her wedding. The well-known difficulties involved in planning such an event gave her an idea for a business. She approached Branson with her idea for a wedding planning business.

Branson gave this business the green light and then some. Virgin Bride was launched in 1996, with Branson, complete with wedding dress, posing for promotional pictures. Virgin is now Europe's largest bridal shop.

This story illustrates another aspect of the Branson style. Admirers and critics alike know about his splashy and outrageous tactics for promotion. He has been compared to P.T. Barnum for his wildly high-visibility promotions. He does not shy away from either controversy or downright tackiness. This attitude makes him loved by some and hated by others, but he is noticed by all, and that's how he likes it.

People can criticise him all they like, Branson is laughing his big toothy laugh all the way to the bank.

Achievements and Foundations

Branson has published his autobiography; *Losing My Virginity: How I've Survived, Had Fun, and Made a Fortune Doing Business My Way* was published in 1998. His book, *Screw It, Let's Do It: Lessons In Life* is a short book that outlines his personal lessons for business and personal success. His lessons here outline the simple principles that have guided him throughout life, many of which were learned from his mother and grandmother. *Business Stripped Bare: Adventures of a Global Entrepreneur* outlines four decades of business success and failure.

His books are a way to share his insights with a wide audience. Branson is known for candour, brashness and openness, and he has no problem sharing his ideas. Branson is a rich source of insight and inspiration.

He became Sir Richard Branson in 1999, knighted for "services to entrepreneurship". Earlier, in 1993, he was awarded an honorary Doctor of Technology degree from Loughborough University. The list of companies involved in the Virgin empire is so numerous that Branson himself is hard-pressed to give an actual number.

Aside from the triumphs in business, Branson has had a notable series of records in adventure sports and travel. He has made several world record attempts with varied success. In 1985, he attempted the fastest crossing of the Atlantic, but capsized early and had to be rescued. The following year, he beat the sailing record.

One year later, he made the fastest balloon crossing of the Atlantic, in the largest balloon, thereby setting two additional records at once. In 1991, he took his balloon across the Pacific, breaking yet another speed record, reaching 394 km/h.

During the years between 1995 and 1998, Branson, along with Steve Fossett and Per Lindstrand, tried to go around the world by balloon. In late 1998, they did complete a record-breaking flight from Morocco to Hawaii. However, they did not complete the global circumnavigation before the record was set by a rival pair of adventurers in 1999.

An entirely different conveyance, an amphibious vehicle, was used in 2004 to set Branson's speed record for such a crossing of the English Channel. He handily beat the previous record by over 4 hours, completing the crossing in 1 h, 40m and 6s.

Branson has also made numerous appearances on television and in print. Many of these are of course profiles and interviews. However, he has been tapped for cameo appearances in movies and on television. The media mogul doesn't miss many chances to appear in the public eye.

Finally, Branson is known for the many philanthropic and other causes that he involves himself with. He has either supported or founded many charities and groups. This tendency showed itself very early in Branson's life, around the time of his first business success. At age 17, he began the Student Valley Centre charity.

Branson is interested in solving the world's biggest problems and thinks that entrepreneurs and leaders have just the right mindset to be able to do so. With that in mind, Branson founded The Elders, an organisation of the world's big achievers devoted to solving big problems. Bringing together the unlikely grouping of politicians to musicians to businessmen, he is not afraid to tackle the biggest questions that society is grappling with. The group includes Nelson Mandela, Desmond Tutu, former US president Jimmy Carter and Peter Gabriel, among others. This group is a fitting gathering. Branson has frequently said that his biggest influences have come from his reading of nonfiction. Nelson Mandela is one of his personal inspirations, and he now has helped to form a mutual admiration society of thinkers that he admires, in order to focus on what he sees as some of the major issues facing everyone.

Other charities include the International Rescue Corps, a group dedicated to search and rescue operations. This group is an independent operation, run completely on donations and volunteer time.

Prisoners Abroad is a group with the goal of helping British citizens who have been detained abroad. The group attempts to assure humane treatment for detainees and to provide support for their families.

Sir Richard is a recipient of the United Nations' Correspondents' Association Citizen of the World Award for supporting these and many other causes.

Sir Richard Branson's Tips for Success

- Given his meteoric and seemingly erratic ventures, one might expect that Branson would have some complicated formulas for business success. Indeed, one might say that a great deal of his strategy is intuitive. Given his academic struggles, because of his dyslexia, he has learned to operate somewhat by "feel". He doesn't read financial reports, being unable to make efficient sense of strings of numbers. He has developed a talent for reading and knowing people. He grasps things in a conceptual way, but often is hard-pressed to quantify things.

- A major key for Sir Richard has been the way that he has turned a disadvantage—his dyslexia—into an advantage. His difficulties with the printed page did not stop him from starting a newspaper. Why not? He understood people, and he is a risk-taker. He realised that having a voice was what the media was about, not typesetting. He hires specialists for each job and understands that the people he hires are the real lifeblood of his enterprises.

- Branson runs his companies with the idea, he says, of "look for the best and you'll get the best." He is a big proponent of providing encouragement to people, in the form of "lavish praise", for motivation. He doesn't run things either by micromanaging or by criticism. "If a flower is watered, it flourishes. If not, it shrivels up and dies. It's much more fun looking for the best in people. People don't need to be told where they've slipped up. They'll sort it out themselves."

> "...look for the best and you'll get the best."

- Notice the word "fun" in Sir Richard's advice. Fun is a major part of the experience for Virgin employees, and this translates into the customer experience. As hard as Branson works, the idea of fun seems to underlie everything he does. One gets the impression that the search for a good time is what really motivates him, and has motivated him his whole life.

- He has mentioned the fact that he thinks that, "Leaders have got to make a bigger effort to make sure that the people who work for them are enjoying what they're doing." Branson himself certainly always seems to be enjoying what he's doing. He relishes big things, big challenges and big accomplishments. One has no trouble imagining that his charisma is infectious enough to sift down through the ranks to his most minor workers.

- He not only communicates with his employees regularly, but shares his thoughts with anyone who cares to listen. He has done many interviews and keeps up a regular blog on his Virgin website. His famous accessibility keeps him in touch with big names and small alike. One sometimes gets the impression that he would chat with just about anyone if he could only find the time.

- He has continued to develop this faculty for risk-taking, coupled with finding people who can create perfection in their own specialties. He himself has mentioned that he cannot grasp how to repair an airplane, but he can find the people who can. When critics said that someone would be foolish to go from the entertainment industry into transportation, he saw the weakness in this argument. He knew he could find the

> "He relishes big things, big challenges and big accomplishments."

engineers for the job, but he also grasped the importance of providing a good experience for passengers, which he exploited by bringing his full experience in the entertainment industry to bear on airline travel.

- Virgin Atlantic is run with the flair that people have come to expect from Branson. The flights offer everything from roomy seating with personal entertainment experiences in economy seating, to the super-luxury of a bar and masseuse in first class.

All of these elements make the adventurer and business buccaneer a continued and dynamic success. He understands the importance of corporate culture. He creates a mood in his companies that keep them self-sustaining and growing. He makes sure that his employees are not just holding a job, but working for something important; their investment in their working time is always something bigger than their tasks. The underdog mentality continues to give everyone something to fight for. Despite the size of his empire, each company has a culture and attitude that they are the little guy and are continually climbing closer to the top.

- On the other hand, this creative, fluid and intuitive attitude works seamlessly with some extremely simple advice for succeeding. Richard Branson makes to-do lists each day. This is one of his basic pieces of advice. Make lists and get them done. The simplicity here can remind us of the importance of fundamentals. Have a goal, break it down into steps and then go out and accomplish each step, one at a time.

> "...get help for mundane tasks whenever possible."

- Such simple, and seemingly obvious, advice underlies a key strategy for Branson— the importance of dedication. If he dedicates himself to a project, he sees it through without loss of focus. His simple advice is to get through the to-do list every day. Consistency in action is the lesson here.

- Finally, Sir Richard advises to get help for mundane tasks whenever possible. He acknowledges the brutal difficulties of trying to start out by doing everything oneself without financial backing. He did have help starting out and getting over some initial hurdles; his mother mortgaged her home to help him in the early days. He has likened his initial investments to going into the equivalent of credit card debt today. He is willing to risk it all on the projects he believes in.

Summary

Sir Richard Branson has a gloriously adventurous attitude no matter what he is doing. He can approach a morning in the office, or a record-setting flight, with the same spirit. He throws himself into things and goes full-bore as if there were no such thing as an obstacle in existence.

What lessons can we take from this? He has certainly lived openly enough to be available as an example for anyone who wants to look to him for ways to create riches and success. His example is one of ambition, adventure, fulfilment and passion. He gives a strong impression of boundless energy.

> "... a laser focus on everything he undertakes."

Let's distil his operating methods down into a few principles:

- Create what you want to see. When Branson looks around at the way things are, he sees what he wishes were there. Then, he goes out and makes these wishes a reality. From his earliest venture, he set out to make something that filled the gulf between what was available at the time and what he wanted.

Student, the paper, was the result of his noticing that young people, including himself, had no real expression and resources with which to speak. Instead of lamenting this lack, he set about creating that means of expression.

- Dedication and consistency are paramount. While Branson is often viewed as a wild card, with his unpredictable moves in business and in life, he doesn't worry as long as things make sense to him. Underlying this apparently mercurial behaviour is really the opposite—a laser focus on everything he undertakes.

He dedicates himself to doing whatever it takes, every single day, to get the job done. So he is an irresistible combination of discipline and risk-taking that elevates entrepreneurship into the level of artistic accomplishment.

> "...doing whatever it takes, every single day, to get the job done."

His utter disregard for all the pitfalls that surround him, coupled with his disciplined push to get things done every day, has rocketed him into the stratosphere of success. This brings us to the next point:

- Never shy away from risks. If Branson demonstrates anything, it is the importance of taking great risks. The real key here is that vision is more important than risk. When he imagines something that he thinks should be created, it happens without regard to what anyone else thinks is the normal course of events.

He has risked his capital and reputation in business, and his life, more than once, in his record-setting sailing and flying attempts. He simply proceeds as if risk were not the point of anything. He has both failed and succeeded with spectacular gusto.

- Set hugely ambitious goals and constantly see if you can surpass them. It would probably never occur to Branson to be afraid that a goal was too big. He would probably be far more bothered by a goal that is too small, deeming it a waste of time.

  He relishes the challenge of setting goals that definitely sound too big. He knows that any goal that is set has an infinitely better chance of success, no matter how outrageous the ambition, than a goal that is never set.

Branson is a stellar example of wealth, success and fulfilment. He has generated billions in wealth, set amazing records and accomplished more in any given year—or month—than most people do in a lifetime. Yet, he is the opposite of the buttoned-up and irritable businessman that we often have as a vague image of the billionaire. His ready smile attests to the joy that a life of accomplishment can bring.

Bill Clinton

"Success is not the measure of a man but a triumph over those who choose to hold him back."

MILLIONAIRES
& BILLIONAIRES

SECRETS
REVEALED!

Brief Overview

Bill Clinton

Born: 19th August, 1946, in Hope, Arkansas, USA

Business: Politics, Public Speaking, 42nd President of the
                 United States of America

Industry: Politics and Public Speaking

Income: $200 million

Lives: Chappaqua, NY, USA

Family: Wife, Hillary, and daughter, Chelsea

Charities: William J. Clinton Foundation, Clinton Climate
                 Initiative

Status: Multimillionaire

Bill Clinton - Former US President

Profile

William Jefferson Clinton was the 42nd president of the United States. He came from obscure and difficult beginnings in the state of Arkansas. He had a rough family background, suffering some abuses in childhood.

Perhaps few would have predicted that a child growing up in rather typically tough circumstances, from a southern US backwater, would rise to a position of world power. That, however, is exactly what Bill Clinton did.

Almost everything that Clinton has done—good and bad—has played out on a large scale. His life is one of well-respected achievement and popularity in many circles. He has partisan supporters all over the world.

This life of ultra-respectable positions has been thoroughly mixed with big scandals, bad behaviour and notoriety. He is a master politician, seemingly coming out clean regardless of the depths to which he has sunk in his private life. Those closest to him usually remain loyal despite their first-hand access to the private scandals.

Clinton's rise to power, despite both difficulty and scandal, has generated plenty of interest. Let's look at his story.

Background

William Jefferson Blythe III was born on 19th August, 1946, in the town of Hope, Arkansas. His inauspicious beginning was made much tougher by the fact that his father, William Jefferson Blythe Jr., a travelling salesman, was killed in an accident three months before Bill's birth.

Bill's mother, Virginia Dell Blythe, remarried while the boy was still young, and the child assumed the surname of Clinton from his stepfather, Roger Clinton, whom his mother married when Bill was 4 years old. This man was both an alcoholic and an abuser. Clinton has said that his stepfather was a drinker and a gambler. Bill claims that Roger's abuse of both Bill's mother and brother were terrible, and Bill intervened many times to stop it. His mother divorced and eventually remarried Roger Clinton, adding to the turbulence of Bill's upbringing.

Before his mother's remarriage, Virginia Dell (maiden name Cassidy) travelled to New Orleans, Louisiana, in order to study nursing. During this time, she left young Bill in the care of her parents, Eldridge and Edith Cassidy. This couple owned a small grocery store and sold goods on credit to blacks in the racially segregated southern US.

After Bill's mother returned and married Roger Clinton, they moved to Hot Springs, Arkansas, where Roger and his brother had an automobile dealership. Young Billy went to St. John's Catholic Elementary School, Ramble Elementary School and then Hot Springs High School.

During these early years, Bill was interested in music and considered making this field his career. He played the saxophone in the state band and was in the chorus. However, he turned his goals toward politics, deciding at age 16 to serve in government office. He notes in his autobiography, "Sometime in my sixteenth year I decided I wanted to be in public life as an elected official. I loved music and thought I could be very good, but I knew I would never be John Coltrane or Stan Getz. I was interested in medicine and thought I could be a fine doctor, but I knew I would never be Michael DeBakey. But I knew I could be great in public service."

Having made his decision, Clinton wasted very little time. In July of 1963, Bill met then-president John F. Kennedy, shortly before his assassination. This helped to cement what Clinton says were early thoughts of, and an interest in, politics as a career. He was afforded this opportunity as a delegate for the Boys Nation program.

Clinton's salvation was his success as a student. He gained academic distinction and qualifications. He attended Georgetown University in Washington, D.C., majoring in international affairs. Clinton was able to attend the school by earning scholarship funds.

He entered politics early, becoming student president during his freshman and sophomore years at Georgetown. During his Junior and Senior years there, he interned for Senator J. William Fulbright of Arkansas. Fulbright was chair of the US Senate Committee on foreign relations. Bill Clinton was an activist who campaigned not only for civil rights, but against the Vietnam War. He was a good match in this for his internship, since Senator Fulbright was also opposed to the war. It was during this internship where he asked for and received the draft deferment that would later mar his reputation during presidential campaigns.

Since these were the Vietnam war years, the military draft was in effect. Clinton approached Senator Fulbright asking for a deferment. Legally, he was a student and could obtain a deferment as a member of the R.O.T.C.

Clinton obtained his Bachelor of Foreign Service degree in 1968. He was able to attend University College at Oxford as a Rhodes

Scholar, leaving the University of Arkansas School of Law in order to do so.

Clinton obtained his law degree from Yale University, graduating in 1973. He then went on to teach, as a member of the faculty of the University of Arkansas School of Law, for the next three years.

> "...youngest man to be elected to any state governorship in the US in 40 years."

During his faculty years, beginning in 1974, he made his first bid for political office, running unsuccessfully for a seat in the United States House of Representatives. The following year he married Hillary Rodham. Hillary also attended Yale Law and was an attorney.

In 1976, Bill Clinton was elected to the office of attorney general of his home state of Arkansas. Two years later, in 1978, he was elected state governor. He was 32 years old and the youngest man to be elected to any state governorship in the US in 40 years.

His first term as governor was contentious and plagued by some unpopular decisions. He raised taxes and fees to fund projects such as the state's infrastructure improvement projects. He campaigned as an incumbent in 1980, but lost this election. This was the same year that Bill and Hillary's only child, Chelsea Clinton, was born.

While Clinton lost the 1980 election, he successfully ran for governor during not only the 1982 election, but was elected successively three more times after that. He only left the governor's seat when he became President of the United States, an office to which he was elected in 1992.

He conducted this campaign while still serving as the Arkansas governor. The pattern of dealing with scandals, with which the world would soon become familiar, began with his presidential bid. These notorious activities are both personal and professional. Clinton's reputation as a womaniser and philanderer dogged him through all of his appointments. Accusations of marijuana use were levelled at Clinton. The "I didn't inhale" claim became a much-touted joke, but didn't seem to seriously harm his reputation. The case of Gennifer Flowers was the first real obstacle. The press caught wind of a long affair with the Arkansas woman. Finally, Bill and Hillary did a widely-watched interview, admitting to some marital struggles, and Clinton's popularity was on the mend. He enjoyed a broad popular appeal as a "regular guy" type.

The avoidance of the draft dogged his campaign as well, but Clinton overcame all of the notoriety to win the highest political seat in the United States. The scandals did not end when Clinton took office. The Whitewater scandal broke in 1994. An investigation was conducted into some financial dealings made by Clinton with a housing development corporation. The investigation failed to come up with conclusive evidence of wrongdoing and Bill Clinton had survived another blow to his reputation. Finally, the Monica Lewinsky story splashed onto headlines, nearly costing him the Oval Office. He was impeached by the House of Representatives, but later tried and found not guilty in the US Senate.

Despite an administration dogged by scandal, questionable decisions, and tawdry behaviour throughout his career, Clinton managed to get elected twice, serving two terms, which is the maximum allowed under US law. This was a major victory for Clinton's Democratic Party, since no Democrat had served two terms in many decades, since the administration of Franklin D. Roosevelt.

The same air of disreputability clings to "Slick Willie" in the post-presidential years. Yet, he manages to be a public and popular figure, finally earning financial success by capitalising on the fame of an ex-president. He continues to be as active in his post-presidential years as he ever was.

Wealth Accumulation

Bill Clinton's financial life has been, in some ways, as rocky as his personal and professional lives. Clinton, in fact, was not a financial success for most of his life. Since he concentrated on public service and political offices, he did not build early wealth in the way that an entrepreneur would have.

He certainly was not born into a class of wealth and privilege. While he did not grow up in conditions of poverty, his family was not among any wealthy elite, being in the business class of life. He grew up in moderate circumstances. He was able to attend expensive educational institutions by earning scholarships and getting other financial help.

> "When he left the white house, he was over $12 million in debt from defending himself against scandals."

He never made more than $US35,000 per year as governor of Arkansas. Even a United States president earns relatively little, considering the stature of the position. When he left the White House, he was over $12 million in debt from defending himself against scandals. Even in his post-presidency, the Clintons were in hot water due to their refusal to release their tax records, until finally succumbing to pressure.

> "He made over $US100 million from the deal for his book and from high personal appearance fees."

Bill Clinton finally made his fortune, within a short time, after his presidential terms. When he left the White House, his income was $358,000, as shown from his tax records. However, the following decade allowed Clinton to finally capitalise on his political career. He made over $US100 million from the deal for his book and from high personal appearance fees.

Clinton is now able to command astronomical income from speaking engagements. As a writer and speaker, the Clinton family income rose to $16 million, in one year, after Clinton left the White House. Since then, the lowest year of income was $7.9 million. This income eventually reached over $20 million in a single year.

Clinton can now command six figures for a single speech. He travels the world making his speaking engagements. He told one audience, "I never had a nickel to my name until I got out of the White House and now I'm a millionaire...."

His book deal reportedly earned him seven figures. In fact, his book income reportedly earned him $29 million, a staggering figure that most authors can never hope to equal in a lifetime.

While most of his career was obviously focused on the rise to power, it is notable that these years of service in politics are far from lucrative for anyone who is serving. Politics is a much easier game for those who have large family incomes.

While, in one sense, Clinton's millions were earned in a few short years, in another sense his wealth has taken him a lifetime to earn. The only reason that he can earn the money that he does for books and speeches is the decades of political life that he has led.

> "I never had a nickel to my name until I got out of the White House and now I'm a millionaire...."

Many of Bill Clinton's speaking engagements are made by wealthy firms. These firms were often supporters of his wife Hillary's early campaigns for the United States Senate. However, he has enjoyed speaking all over the world, from Ireland to Australia.

His appeal as a speaker has lasted well beyond his presidential years. He is able to maintain his prestige and popularity among an international audience. This is due as much to his having attained the status of a celebrity as to the fact that he is a former US president. It is a bit of a mystery why or how Clinton manages this and it is often explained as the "Clinton mystique".

There are several reasons why Clinton remains a popular figure. One is the simple fact that he is a master politician, which is the art of making oneself publicly visible. He has been practicing this art from a very young age. As was already noted, he decided to go into the political game at the tender age of 16, so he has cultivated his talents for speaking since then.

> "Clinton is a charismatic and dynamic figure."

He might also have his wife to thank for part of this visibility. When Bill Clinton left his high public office, Hillary had already begun making her bids for political positions of her own. This continuing public visibility lends the power couple an air of ongoing dynamism that keeps them in the spotlight.

The hint of scandal that clings to him offers support for the notion that there is no such thing as bad publicity. While there is no shortage of serious speaking engagements, he gets plenty of attention from the press simply for being the large-scale colourful character that he is. The media continues to pay attention to Bill Clinton.

He stays involved with many projects that lend weight to his public image. He heads up or contributes to so many international projects, including many public projects, that he maintains his credibility as a diplomatic figure.

Many people maintain their admiration and liking for Bill Clinton. It seems that, no matter how much wrongdoing or scandal follows him, his supporters are ready to follow him, too. There is no denying that Clinton is a charismatic and dynamic figure. He has a talent for drawing both attention and loyalty, in spite of it all.

This perpetual popularity has, at last, translated into wealth for Clinton. $100 million is not bad when considered as a lifetime income. When one thinks about the fact that this income was made in a decade, one realises the impact of his words on the world.

He has a talent for denying and being circumspect, and then, on a dime, being very unabashed in a single public appearance. He can be humorous and charming. He once said about his autobiography, "A lot of presidential memoirs, they say, are dull and self-serving. I hope mine is interesting and self-serving." This winking attitude provides some clue to Clinton's appeal. He can be at once sincere and tongue-in-cheek.

Clinton has an eye for current events, of course, and for popular causes. He has devoted himself to these since he left the office of president. It is fitting that he can now work for these causes, to which he has devoted his life, and finally make an income that reflects all of his hard work.

It is difficult to tell whether money is really important to Bill Clinton. As we have noted, for most of his life he managed just fine—to say the least—with very little. His attention was focused on another kind of progress entirely. He concentrated completely on moving from one political office to another, higher one.

On the other hand, he is no doubt enjoying his wealth now. After all, it really represents the accumulated rewards of the many years spent working in political office. There is no good reason why he should not cash in on that work at last.

Plenty of his current large income is not kept for personal use. He gives plenty of money to charity, supporting his own and other causes. He certainly has accumulated enough wealth to live comfortably, and he does. But Clinton and his wife continue to work on other priorities. Clinton has never claimed to be good with money. He has said, "On the ...money...all that stuff...I'm the bad guy. All this stuff is kept away from me." While Clinton has at last struck it rich, his success has been in the areas of power and influence rather than dollars.

Achievements and Foundations

Bill Clinton's rise to power was steady and forceful. He went into politics early and seems to have focused on nothing else. Clinton's achievements have been stellar and public. His early notable achievements were mostly academic. Becoming a Rhodes Scholar puts Clinton among a tiny handful of the academic elite. He began his ascent after getting his degree and simply did not stop until he could go no higher.

During his presidency, Clinton was credited with any number of achievements. He is widely regarded for bringing peace to Ireland and many people openly admire him for this action as president. This earned him acclaim far outside of the US.

He signed the Family and Medical Leave Act of 1993 not long after assuming the president's office. This act required large companies to allow workers to take a maternity or other medical leave, and enjoyed wide popular support.

Despite the scandals, Clinton left office with one of the highest approval ratings of any modern exiting president. His 68% ratings were on a par with those of Ronald Regan and his Democratic two-term predecessor, Franklin D. Roosevelt. Those numbers indicated that even many people who didn't like him still thought that he did a good job as president. The self-described "comeback kid" has returned over and over again.

Since then, his life has been taken up with activism, which keeps him in the international spotlight. He is still very active in political affairs, endorsing various candidates, including his wife Hillary in her unsuccessful bid for the Democratic presidential run against eventual winner Barack Obama.

After leaving office in 2002, Clinton returned to his home state of Arkansas to leave a legacy. The William J. Clinton Presidential Center and Park was dedicated and opened in the city of Little Rock. This houses the Clinton Presidential Library. The building is also home to the Clinton School of Public Service, and the Clinton Foundation offices.

He started the William J. Clinton Foundation, whose projects include the HIV/AIDS Initiative. This project makes efforts to test and treat the disease in poor parts of the world. Clinton's organisation, in part, aims to work with medical companies in order to reduce the costs of medicines being delivered to the third world. The Foundation also makes efforts to combat childhood obesity in wealthier nations.

Under the umbrella of the William J. Clinton Foundation is also the Clinton Climate Initiative, or CCI. This branch of the Foundation takes its place among the current green activism projects. Its aim is to improve energy efficiency and to halt deforestation.

He is also founder of the Clinton Global Initiative, which is an organisation dedicated to bringing together world leaders and private executives to organise social improvement efforts.

He has also put his energy into other efforts, including freeing journalist prisoners and helping hurricane relief.

After the Indian Ocean tsunami disaster, Clinton served as a special envoy for relief efforts in the area until 2007. He was appointed as a special envoy to Haiti in 2009, joining Bush in efforts to bring relief to sufferers of a devastating earthquake.

He followed former US president George Bush as chairman of the National Constitution Center, which is a Philadelphia history museum.

Clinton published his autobiography, *My Life*, in 2004. He also wrote *Giving: How Each of Us Can Change the World* in 2007.

Clinton has been honoured in myriad ways. These praises come from a wide variety of sources. They range from statues to schools bearing his name, from honorary degrees to the International Freedom Conductor Award for his efforts after the tsunami.

> "It's how you handle adversity, not how it affects you."

Clinton is even the proud possessor of a Grammy Award, the entertainment award for musicians. Clinton might have dreamed of winning a Grammy if he had pursued the musical career that he thought about as a schoolboy. The award actually was the result of his project of narrating an album containing Wolf Tracks and Peter and the Wolf, a production of the Russian National Orchestra. The award was for Best Spoken Word Album for Children and Clinton accompanied Mikhail Gorbachev and Sophia Loren in telling the stories.

Bill Clinton's Tips for Success

- "Big things are expected of us, and nothing big ever came of being small." Clinton set his sights high from an early age. He achieved success by thinking big and shooting for distinction during his school years. He reached the ranks of elite scholars by the time he was going for his postgraduate education. This is the product of simple hard work and a clear-cut goal. He was focused on what he wanted, and he kept going until he attained it. He certainly has not stopped to this day. Even a major heart operation has hardly slowed him down.

> "... never quit, never quit, never quit."

- "If you live long enough, you'll make mistakes. But if you learn from them, you'll be a better person. It's how you handle adversity, not how it affects you. The main thing is never quit, never quit, never quit."

This statement reflects an attitude that is necessary to overcome obstacles. It isn't as important what happens to you, as what you do about it. And "never quit" is simple enough, but it makes the difference between success and failure.

> "None of Clinton's very public mistakes were excuses for him to fail."

None of Clinton's very public mistakes were excuses for him to fail. He has dealt with them all in a public manner, as he needed to do. He does whatever is necessary to put mistakes behind him and to keep moving forward. While his story is rife with misdeeds, there is a lesson in this for all of us. We can take comfort from Clinton's mistakes. He has made some major ones and has done it all in the public eye. Yet, not

> "Success is not the measure of a man but a triumph over those who choose to hold him back."

one of those was an insurmountable obstacle to him.

If he can overcome those mistakes, we can all face our own failures and go on to succeed.

• "Success is not the measure of a man but a triumph over those who choose to hold him back."

This enigmatic quote illustrates the ruthlessness necessary to rise to the top of the heap. As harsh as it may sound, it is yet another lesson from Clinton on overcoming obstacles. Not only should nothing stand in your way if you want to succeed, no one should be allowed to stand in your way. There are people who will encourage us to fail, either deliberately or inadvertently. Obviously, if you have political opponents, there are people who are definitely trying to hold you back. Clinton's sense of this, and determination to rise above it, is part of what allowed him to ignore the things that people put in his way.

Even for people who are not in politics, other people sometimes do stand in the way. Envy of success might play a part here, but often people simply don't believe that achievement is possible. This can be just as true of ourselves as it is of the people that we interact with. If we want to succeed, no one, including ourselves, should stand in our way.

- "Sometimes, when people are under stress, they hate to think and it's the time when they most need to think."

> "Sometimes, when people are under stress, they hate to think and it's the time when they most need to think."

Clinton has pushed to take the most high-pressure of positions. When under pressure, the person that can keep their head is the one who comes out on top. This statement of Clinton's contains a very important lesson. The ability to handle stressful situations well is often not discussed as a major contributor to success, but it should be an integral part of any strategy.

Some people, in fact many of us, stop in the face of feeling overwhelmed and pressured. When a job seems too big, it is tempting to set our sights lower, or to choose another path. But a task that seems overwhelming might just be the one that will lead to great success.

All of our stories here focus on people who make big

things happen. With big success comes big stressors, especially on the climb to the top. Perhaps the difference between these major success stories and the more average life lies, at least in part, in the ability to think under pressure.

- "We should, all of us, be filled with gratitude and humility for our present progress and prosperity. We should be filled with awe and joy at what lies over the horizon. And we should be filled with absolute determination to make the most of it."

This attitude is the complement to the reference to adversity. There are more than obstacles to be overcome on the road to success and riches. There are also opportunities that surround us all the time, which are ignored or taken for granted. In order to get ahead in life, these things must be appreciated and taken advantage of.

- "We cannot build our own future without helping others to build theirs." Clinton's whole career has been focused on the idea of interdependence. He believes that success is built on helping others.

Bill Clinton does know how to succeed. He has been a success despite many disadvantages, obstacles and errors. Through it all, he simply keeps going. Clinton's life shows how the advantage of making your way by earning an excellent education can pave the way for success in life. While we cannot all be Rhodes Scholars, or graduates of Yale Law, we can all take advantage of educational opportunities.

You're doing this right now by taking action and reading this book; I guarantee you'll be smarter and further along the road to wealth and success from having read this book.

Clinton worked extremely hard in school and his hard work paid off in a big way. He took full advantage of his educational years. He not only achieved the distinction that allowed him to be admitted into top schools. He also joined organisations and ran for student leadership offices in the meantime.

> "Success is ultimately the result of work."

His behaviour illustrates his drive to take advantages of the opportunities afforded by social organisation. He joined a fraternity in college and joined the Youth Order of DeMolay. He never became a fully-fledged Freemason, but he was elected to other fraternities. He was an active member of social organisations, such as those dedicated to opposing the Vietnam War.

All of these activities point out another major quality that allowed for Bill Clinton's enormous success. His energy is seemingly boundless. He is constantly working, meeting people, associating, and organising. We might not all have the natural energy to copy him, but we can take note of the tremendous impact of being active. Success is ultimately the result of work. Work, quite simply, takes energy. This applies to human activity just as strictly as it does in principles of physics.

Clinton is a tireless campaigner, and not only on the political trail. He seems to be constantly working and scheming for other projects and to expand his own interests and opportunities. Working that hard simply must pay off in the long run.

Many of the people who change the world seem to be perpetual-motion machines and Bill Clinton is no exception. This man's energy seems to affect everyone around him and his success is due in large part to this capacity for work.

His stamina shows the importance, not simply of physical energy, but of persistence. The former president impresses one as a man who has not flagged since the day he was born.

Finally, Clinton highlights the importance of being both a man of his times and a man opposed to his times. He was the first president of the post-baby-boom era, and grew up during a time of great change. He not only learned about the important issues of the day, he became immersed in causes. He learned to listen, and to understand what people were thinking, and he developed his own opinions.

When Clinton found a cause to support, he dove in head-first. He took action both inside and outside of the system. This dynamic combination made him a man who was both in touch with his times and someone who was pushing to change the status quo.

This attitude is an obvious asset—probably a necessity, in fact—when it comes to politics. Outside the political arena, though, the idea can still create success. In order for a person to create something and make a mark, they should understand the way things are and what ideas are dominant. However, it is also important to be able to visualise the way things should be, and to be capable of taking steps to make the changes that a person wants to see in the world. The creative interplay between these two visions—the way things are and the way they could be—is a formula for initiative.

Summary

What lessons can be learned from the success of Bill Clinton? His was a long and winding road to riches. His wealth was actually secondary—the result of capitalising on other achievements. His example actually shows the road to power and influence. So, how did he do it?

First of all, Clinton is an expert political operator. He understands the system and he works it to his advantage. He knows that reputation is not as important as it might seem in the political arena. Popular appeal is more important than a squeaky-clean image. He has attained this with a combination of brazenness and hard work.

Politics is not for the faint of heart. Clinton has been able to weather any number of storms and is a tremendous example of persistence. He faced early challenges with his stepfather. He was moved around from his mother to his grandparents and back to his mother as a child, but his vision seems to have been steady and grounded.

Bill Clinton ensured his own success by understanding the importance of his educational background. He worked hard in school and paid attention to achieving distinction. He was dogged in his pursuits and was rewarded with meeting President Kennedy while still in high school. From there, his success with student organisations and academic awards continued to mount. With this academic road went the formation of personal connections that helped him throughout his career.

Finally, Clinton's associates all note that he has tremendous energy and stamina. He simply keeps working and working. He continues to pursue his goals day in, day out, year after year.

This is how Bill Clinton achieved dizzying heights of power with his drive, energy and connections that he built during his formative years.

Oprah Winfrey

*"If you want your life to be more rewarding,
you have to change the way you think."*

OPRAH WINFREY NETWORK

MILLIONAIRES & BILLIONAIRES

SECRETS REVEALED!

Brief Overview

Oprah Winfrey

Born: 29th January, 1954, in Kosciusko, Mississippi, USA

Business: Talk Show Host, Media Proprietor

Industry: Television

Income: Salary $385 million. net worth $2.4 billion

Lives: Chicago, Illinois, USA

Family: Partner, Stedman Graham.

Charities: Oprah's Angel Network, various others

Status: Billionaire

Profile

Oprah Winfrey is one of the world's most stellar—and public—success stories. Her reign in television and publishing has been of astonishing duration. She has taken the daytime talk show into areas that go well beyond the formulaic structure of other shows. She is one of the most popular media figures in the US and around the world.

Like some of the other stories in this book, she came from the proverbial poverty and obscurity situation to become a media mogul. She is a classic rags-to-riches story. Hers is an excellent example of the underdog who ends up winning big.

Oprah has been famously open about her life, history and opinions. She has made no effort to hide her past. In fact, she has told her story to her entire worldwide audience. Part of her success rests on her honesty, sincerity and utter transparency.

She has built up a powerhouse of media and publishing success under her Harpo company name. All of her holdings carry the stamp that makes Oprah special. Hers is a brand that connotes quality, big thinking and the sincerity that is characteristic of the woman who has lived as part of the media, but without the stain of disreputability that many media figures carry. Agree with her views or not, she brings some grace and presence to the game of entertainment meets news media.

Background

Oprah Winfrey was born on 29 January, 1954, in Kosciusko, Mississippi, USA. She was actually christened "Orpah" after a biblical figure. However, people began calling her "Oprah" early on, and this is the name that stuck with her.

She was born to an unmarried mother and had difficult beginnings. Her mother was a maid, Vernita Lee. Her father was Vernon Winfrey, who was serving in the military when Oprah was born. They were both teenagers at the time and never married. There is, in fact, some doubt that the man that she knew as her father was really in fact her biological parent, since another man, Noah Robinson Sr., later claimed to have fathered her child. In any case, Vernita Lee and Vernon Winfrey were young and broke up before Oprah was born.

Soon after Oprah's birth, her mother sent her baby to live with her grandmother, Hattie Mae Lee, where she was raised until the age of 6. This start in life was at one and the same time very difficult and an excellent foundation.

Hattie Mae lived in rural Mississippi. The conditions surrounding a poor, black, southern child in America at this time meant that Oprah's early years were spent in almost unimaginable poverty. There was no electricity and no plumbing. Oprah and her grandmother made do on the barest necessities.

Despite the hardships, Oprah credits her grandmother with saving her life. Hattie Mae placed an emphasis on education, teaching Oprah to read when she was three years old. Her grandmother's strict methods provided Oprah with a good start to her schooling.

Hattie Mae raised Oprah until she was 6. After that, Oprah went back to live with her mother in Milwaukee, Wisconsin. Her living situation here was particularly rough in many ways, even though the general living conditions might have been considered slightly less harsh than the situation with her grandmother.

Even though Oprah was now living in a more developed city, the parental attention she received from her mother was far more neglectful than her previous situation. Vernita Lee was working long hours as a housemaid and Oprah was surrounded by some bad influences in Milwaukee. Much later in life, Oprah revealed that she suffered through sexual molestation, starting at the age of 9. A 19-year-old cousin sexually abused her, and convinced Oprah to keep the rape a secret. The abuse did not stop here, because Oprah was later sexually molested by an uncle and also by a friend of her mother's.

The years of nightmarish living took their toll on the young Oprah. The abusive attention caused trauma and confusion in the young girl. She began a pattern of rebellious behaviour, becoming promiscuous and intractable. Winfrey tried to run away from

> "Her love of books and learning blossomed"

home at the age of 13. Her mother attempted to place her in a detention centre, but she was turned away because the facility was full. Finally, at the age of 14, she was sent to live with her father, Vernon, in Nashville, Tennessee. During this same year, Winfrey had become pregnant. She gave birth to a baby who died shortly thereafter.

Winfrey's situation improved after she went to live with Vernon. Oprah's father was an extremely strict, but loving and encouraging parent. Her father's influence, and no doubt her own self-motivation, began to assert itself in her later teen years. Oprah says that she knew that there was far more out there in the world than had been her experience up until then. She had read about the wider world, and was determined to reach for better things.

Oprah Winfrey thrived under the tutelage of her father. Oprah tells of the way in which her father insisted that she read one book, and write a book report, each week while she lived there. It was as if Vernon picked up where Oprah's grandmother had left off. Her love of books and learning blossomed, and she began to flourish at school.

Oprah attended East Nashville High School, and began to distinguish herself academically and socially. She became an honours student, joined the speech team, worked in a grocery store and was voted Most Popular Girl.

Oprah was also a lovely girl. She won a beauty pageant at the age of 17, the Miss Black Tennessee competition. She entered broadcasting early, landing a job at a local radio station during her senior year in high school, a position that she held for three years. In addition, she won a scholarship to Tennessee State University by winning a competition for oratory.

Oprah, true to form, studied Speech Communication and Performing Arts while at Tennessee State. She had been used to speaking in public from a very early age, another legacy of her grandmother's influence. She obtained her degree in 1976.

She had started her career as a reporter in Nashville, Tennessee, with the radio station WVOL, in high school. She worked here during her first two years of college. After that, she signed on as a reporter and news anchor in television, beginning her position at WTVF-TV, also in Nashville. While she says that she never felt comfortable as a reporter, she never left television. After graduating in 1976, Winfrey accepted a co-anchor chair for WJZ-TV in Baltimore, Maryland. This turned out to be a key move for Winfrey. She was the youngest anchor on the show, and the first black woman to hold this position. Two years after beginning this job, she was offered the position of co-host of a morning show called "People Are Talking". It was in this position that

Oprah first got a taste of the talk-show format, and where her style of self-expression began to develop.

In 1984, Oprah changed positions, moving to Chicago to host the morning talk show "AM Chicago". When she began, this show was at the bottom of the ratings, but Oprah brought her already-strong presence to bear on the show. Within a few short months, the show went to the number one spot. This talk show ousted the popular Donohue show for the highest-ranked talk show in Chicago. It was renamed the Oprah Winfrey show in 1985, the year after Winfrey took the helm. The show was so hot that, a year later, "The Oprah Winfrey Show" went into national US syndication. Once again, Oprah took the show to the #1 spot within a year, this time in front of a national television audience. Extraordinarily, it has remained there, at the top of the talk-show heap, ever since. *The Oprah Winfrey Show* remains the most highly-rated daytime talk show in history.

> *"The Oprah Winfrey Show* remains the most highly-rated daytime talk show in history."

Just before the talk show reached a national audience, Oprah cemented her high place with audiences with a launch onto the big screen. She had landed a role in the hit movie *The Color Purple*, and won critical acclaim for her first acting performance as Sofia, a role which she made her own. This role was so coveted by Winfrey that she has later told audiences that she was obsessed with playing the part. It was a big opportunity for an untried actress, because it was a big-budget film from Steven Spielberg. The 1985 release earned her Best Supporting Actress nominations at the Academy and Golden Globe awards.

Although she did not win these awards, the combination of her personal popularity as a show host and her strong movie performance provided a one-two punch that made Oprah Winfrey a famous name as soon as she was ready to take the stage in front of a wide audience.

Wealth Accumulation

Oprah's extraordinary wealth and success began with her success as a television host. She was, as you might imagine, increasingly well-paid as her ratings went up. When

> "'Harpo' is Oprah spelled backwards."

The Oprah Winfrey Show went national, she attained millionaire status. She was reportedly earning $2 million a year by the late 1980s from her show.

Oprah did not stop with the idea of a comfortable salary. She expanded her media success into a media empire. The show was so successful that Winfrey was able to go into business on the production side of things. She started Harpo productions. "Harpo" is Oprah spelled backwards. The quirky name is rather oddly poetic, since Harpo was also the name of the character that was Sophia's husband in the movie *The Color Purple*. The movie and the production company bookend Winfrey's rise to fame and fortune.

Oprah first negotiated ownership of her own show. She then expanded the production company. Harpo has not only expanded to become a media powerhouse for Oprah herself, but has launched many other careers as well. Oprah is constantly on the lookout for new talent. When she finds someone that she thinks is promising, she nurtures their careers.

Oprah Winfrey met Dr. Phil McGraw under unusual circumstances in 1998. Her show was by then so influential that one of her shows had affected the entire cattle industry, and a suit was filed against her. Dr. McGraw's company, Courtroom Sciences, Inc., was hired to help during the Texas state trial. Oprah was impressed enough by the doctor to ask him to come on her show. He appeared as a regular favourite for a few years. Winfrey decided to back him with his own show, and Harpo Productions launched *Dr. Phil* in 2002. Oprah Winfrey has made many careers, but Dr. Phil was just the first to gain a hit show under her aegis and specifically supported by her.

Others were to follow. Television cook Rachael Ray was spotted by Oprah and brought on the show. She received a huge boost to her audience with the official blessing of Winfrey, the media powerhouse. Once again, Winfrey's Harpo Productions launched a successful daily show with Rachael Ray.

The Dr. Oz Show followed. Oprah was by now following a familiar pattern. She would begin by finding a guest that she liked to have on her show. Dr. Oz was brought on to answer health questions from viewers and Oprah herself. His interesting presentations became a popular regular feature on *Oprah*, and then the doctor had his own show launched by Harpo. Dr. Phil, Rachael Ray, and Dr. Oz are all now successful television hosts. Oprah and her protégés have all made smashing successes on daytime TV. Oprah has a great talent to make money for herself, and to help other talents that she discovers along the way. She is scheduled to launch a show for her final popular protégé, designer Nate Berkus, in the Fall 2010 season.

In addition to these shows, Harpo has other projects and companies. Harpo Films, Inc. is the company's largest division. This company is based in the film mecca of Los Angeles, rather than in Winfrey's Chicago studios. The company produces many films, particularly for television.

Harpo Radio, Inc. produces the satellite radio channel entitled Oprah & Friends. Oprah's long-time friends and most popular guests have regular features on the channel.

Harpo Studios is the division that produces Oprah's show, which is still her central and most distinguished product. The studio is set to produce a channel that will take the place of cable's Discovery Health Channel in 2011.

By the early 1990s, she made more money than any other woman in the entertainment industry. By the mid-1990s, she made the *Forbes 400* list of richest people. Oprah was the only black person on the list, and remains one of the only black people to have remained on that list almost every year since.

> "By the mid-1990s, she made the *Forbes 400* list of richest people."

She owns "*O*", the Oprah Magazine, and is the co-founder of Oxygen Media, which has a channel on cable television.

She has also successfully acted in movie roles in addition to *The Color Purple*, further increasing her prestige and fortune.

Oprah became the first black female in the US to reach billionaire status. She may have been the first black female billionaire ever. She reached billionaire status in 2004, and continues to reign on Forbes' list of the world's select few billionaires. Oprah Winfrey took her place among the wealthy of the earth. She earns over $300 million each year. Some estimates have noted that doing her show provides Winfrey an income of over half a million US dollars per day.

Oprah seems able to do no wrong, in her earning power as well as in her reputation. Even the recent economic downturn affected Winfrey very little, compared to other fortune-makers. Her popular appeal holds in good times and in bad, making her relatively recession-proof.

Oprah Winfrey has the true Midas touch. She has not suffered the wild ups and downs of many builders of fortunes. These rises and falls usually form part and parcel of the risk-taking inherent in making big money. Oprah, however, has made a steady rise, with each new success bigger than the last.

> "Oprah became the first black female in the US to reach billionaire status."

Oprah Winfrey is a highly-paid person even in the moneyed world of entertainment. She has found a formula for success that seems bulletproof.

She has put herself on the line in order to earn her wealth. Her empire is built on her personality and life in a way that few other success stories are. Any entrepreneur must put heart and soul into an enterprise that they are passionate about.

> "She earns over $300 million each year."

However, Winfrey gives new meaning to this idea. From her early days, she has earned her success by putting her own stories, ideas and feelings on the line. She probably has precious few secrets from the public by now. She is, indeed, far too famous to keep things hidden anymore. Even past difficulties have been leaked or raked up when she would rather keep these things private.

> "...half a million US dollars per day."

But she is not a very private personality in many ways. She has succeeded in the way she has due to her willingness to put herself out into the public spotlight, not merely as a celebrity, but as the Oprah/Harpo soul, face and heart. Her massive appeal is due to the fact that she can relate to almost anyone, and does not spare herself in an effort to do so.

Her famous sincerity and heartfelt honesty have brought confessions and private feelings out of her guests in front of worldwide television audiences. Oprah herself has also made personal revelations throughout her career. While this occasionally earns some scorn and ridicule

> "Her massive appeal is due to the fact that she can relate to almost anyone."

from some quarters, her massive audiences find this to be the very quality that they admire in her. Her sincere openness has meant pure gold, both for watchers and for Winfrey herself.

Forbes confirms that Oprah Winfrey is the "richest woman in entertainment", surpassing even the biggest movie actresses, who can command close to $20 million for each film performance. Even the recession-resistant Oprah's worth has undergone fluctuations recently, but she still manages to remain the only black female billionaire. Recent estimates have placed the media mogul's fortune at figures varying anywhere from $1.5 to $2.6 billion US.

Achievements and Foundations

Oprah Winfrey's earlier achievements included winning a beauty contest (Miss Black Tennessee) at age 17, her college scholarship, and her early rise to fame with her interview show.

Since then, she has had a series of highly influential and large-scale projects. Her book club can make best-sellers. She brought Barack Obama to national attention when she endorsed him, although she afterward tried to distance herself from the campaign in order to allow the candidate to run without her influence.

Winfrey has garnered many honours and accolades. Starting in the mid-1990s, her awards have become increasingly prestigious. She won the Gold Medal Award from the International Radio & Television Society Foundation. She became a George Foster Peabody Award winner for Individual Achievement. She was awarded a 50th Anniversary Gold Medal from The National Book Foundation.

The Oprah Winfrey Show alone has won over 40 Daytime Emmy Awards®. Over 20 of these were in the categories relating to Creative Arts. Seven were for Outstanding Host and nine were awarded for Outstanding Talk Show. All of the above awards were bestowed before 1998. That year, Oprah won the Lifetime Achievement Award from the National Academy of Television Arts & Sciences, after which she withdrew herself from consideration for any further Emmys. In 2000, her show removed itself as well. No one knows how many might have followed in over a decade had she not done this.

1998 was also the first year that *Time Magazine* put Winfrey on its list of the 100 Most Influential People of the 20th Century. She would later make the periodical's 100 Most Influential People in the World list, starting in 2004. She has remained on this list every year since then, the only person to have done so.

> "Winfrey in on its list of the 100 Most Influential People of the 20th Century."

Many of Winfrey's accolades have been won for her charitable efforts, as well. She was awarded the Bob Hope Humanitarian Award at The Emmys in 2002. She is also the recipient of the United Nations Association of the United States of America Global Humanitarian Action Award. She also has the 2005 National Freedom Award from the National Civil Rights Museum, is a Hall of Fame honouree from the National Association for the Advancement of Colored People, and won the 2007 Humanitarian Award from The Elie Weisel Foundation for Humanity.

Those awards are due to the fact that she makes a major philanthropic contribution through numerous projects and donations.

Oprah's Angel Network moved onto a worldwide stage. This organisation coordinated many different charitable efforts, and the full force of Winfrey's name provided the publicity. Everything from a school in Africa to homes rebuilt after hurricane Katrina fall under the purview of the Angel Network. The network was set up to coordinate charitable giving efforts from Oprah's viewers and friends. Part of Winfrey's overall approach is to spread good things, and she makes many efforts to encourage charity. The Angel Network was set up so that 100% of all contributions went to the designated charities. Oprah herself paid all of the administrative expenses of running the foundation in order to ensure that this happened. Over the course of a decade, the Angel Network had collected over 80 million dollars. The funds went to many charities. These charities were mostly focused on bringing educational opportunities to kids, in order to educate future world leaders. Since *The Oprah Winfrey Show* is due to wrap up its impressive run in 2011, the Angel Network is now closed to donations. Winfrey will continue to encourage giving to charity through her new OWN cable network (OWN stands for the Oprah Winfrey Network).

Winfrey herself is one of the most generous of American philanthropists, with the reported total private donations coming from Winfrey totalling $41 million in a single year in addition to her other money-raising efforts.

> "...private donations coming from Winfrey totalling $41 million in a single year."

In addition, she still runs other large charitable projects. The mission of the Oprah Winfrey Foundation is to "support the inspiration, empowerment and education of women, children, and families around the world".

The project that is closest to Winfrey's heart is the Oprah Winfrey Leadership Academy and the Academy Foundation that runs the charitable effort. Winfrey set up the school to provide opportunities for girls living in the poverty-stricken conditions of South Africa. The school was founded and overseen by Winfrey personally. She even had a part in hand-picking each student— girls that she felt had the potential to change the world if they were given the proper education. She says that, "The school will teach girls to be the best human beings they can ever be; it will train them to become decision-makers and leaders; it will be a model school for the rest of the world." It has been reported that, once the show's run ends, Oprah will spend part of her time living in her own house on the school grounds.

The pain of abuse that Oprah Winfrey endured as a child has in part fuelled her activist work to this day. Most of her charity work focuses on improving the conditions and educational opportunities for children all over the world. She also is active in attempting to work on legal measures that would help to reduce the incidence of child abuse. She was instrumental in getting the National Child Protection Act ("Oprah's Bill) passed as US law. The act establishes a national registry of convicted child abusers, facilitating law enforcement investigation and prosecution of abusers.

Winfrey is hugely influential, and any cause that she decides to put the force of her name behind garners tremendous attention. She is extremely active in philanthropic work. She accomplishes as much as she does by attempting to get everyone involved. She devotes some of her shows to highlighting the issues that she finds important, and encourages friends and fans alike to participate in any way they can. Her inclusive attitude runs seamlessly together with her other show subjects, since her style and persona have always been heartfelt.

Many people have credited Winfrey with tremendous influence. She has been called the most influential woman in the world by more than one person. When she expresses an opinion, millions of people listen.

Agree or disagree with her views, there is no doubt that she has a large following, and her opinions matter. At the very least, she puts the power of her voice behind the causes that she believes in.

No one who makes it big ever goes through life without controversy. Winfrey attracts highly partisan reactions. She has admirers and detractors alike. There are many people who scoff at the devotion that she seems to inspire. However, there is no doubt that she does inspire such devotion, and that says plenty about her force of character.

Oprah Winfrey's Tips for Success

Ms. Winfrey stresses passion for what you are doing as the key to success. She has governed her life by doing and talking about the things that she strongly believes in. She seems to hardly have made a misstep, given the number of people who hang on her every word. Doing the things that she believes in has made Oprah billions.

> **"Doing the things that she believes in has made Oprah billions."**

- Oprah says to do what you love, "and the rest will come". Following one's passions is a recurring theme throughout this book, but Oprah just might be the prime example. This is due to the fact that her beliefs and passions have not only guided the building of her empire, in one sense, they are her empire. Ms. Winfrey has made a career of expressing what she thinks, and of coaxing others' thoughts out of them too.

> **"The big secret in life is that there is no big secret."**

- She also says, "You know you're doing the right thing when you would do what you do even if you weren't getting paid for it." This is true passion. If you would do what you do as a hobby, and turn it into a career, you will always have passion behind your work.

- So, what is the secret to living a successful life? "The big secret in life is that there is no big secret. Whatever your goal, you can get there if you're willing to work."

Is it possible that the great achievers of the world *don't* possess some secret knowledge that the rest of us are not privy to? Over and over again, we see that the world's entrepreneurs and other giant success stories speak in very simple principles when they are asked about how they succeeded. Perhaps the big secret is that they can, and do, break their goals down into simple principles, and they never lose sight of them.

Winfrey touches on a very important thought here. There is no big secret. Instead, she mentions two ideas here that apply to every big success story. One idea is goals, and the other is hard work.

These are the keys to achievement. A goal or vision, one that remains unchanged and important in its essentials, provides focus. The work is what brings us closer. Being successful and wealthy is the end result of focusing on one clear goal and working toward it every single day.

- Would Oprah herself interpret her statement that way? She says, "Energy is the essence of life. Every day you decide how you're going to use it by knowing what you want and what it takes to reach that goal and by maintaining focus." This, once again, highlights those simple ideas—energy (to put in the hard work), having a goal and focusing on that goal.

- Looking at her story, and listening to Oprah, one can easily get the impression that nothing she does ever really fails. How is this possible? She says, "I do not believe in failure. It is not failure if you enjoyed the process." This is yet another way of saying to do what you love and the rest will follow. No matter what mistakes are made, or what short-term obstacles might rise in a person's path, enjoying the process will provide motivation to keep going until success is the result.

- "The key to realising a dream is to focus not on success but significance, and then even the small steps and little victories along your path will take on greater meaning." By now, it is more than clear that Oprah Winfrey is driven every waking moment to do things that she believes in. She does things that she thinks are important, and success is the result, not the motivation.

- How does a person overcome obstacles? "Do the one thing you think you cannot do. Fail at it. Try again. Do better the second time. The only people who never tumble are those who never mount the high wire. This is your moment. Own it."

> "...the importance of risking failure. Success is not possible without it."

So, it's not that Oprah has some magic power that protects her from failure. She simply keeps trying until she succeeds, regardless of what happens on her first try. In fact, this points out the importance of risking failure. Success is not possible without it. People who achieve big things do not do so by avoiding failure. They achieve by trying, failing, and trying again until they can make it work.

- "My philosophy is that not only are you responsible for your life, but doing the best at this moment puts you in the best place for the next moment." We can see a recurring theme in statements, not just from Ms. Winfrey, but from other people who have made it big. No matter what they do, they do *something*. They simply put in their best effort toward their goals, day in and day out. They do not postpone, they take action.

- "You can have it all. You just can't have it all at once." Oprah Winfrey's own ideas about having it all are goals, not wishes. She doesn't try to do everything at the same time, but she does achieve ever greater goals and reach higher and higher things. She understands that accomplishments come only when you work for them, and it's all right if they come singly.

- "We are each responsible for our own life – no other person is or even can be." This is not the only time that Oprah has made a statement about this important idea. She says that she realised from a very young age that only she was responsible for her own life, and that she knew that she had to make good. It is significant that we never hear a self-made person make excuses or place blame on others for failures. They simply take responsibility for everything. This notion is what allows them to be in control of their own success, because they take responsibility for every action.

> "...simply take responsibility for everything."

Summary

So, what are the main lessons that we can learn from Oprah Winfrey's story? She has been such a spectacular success that there are many lessons to be gleaned about building both wealth and self-fulfillment from her. But, as always, we can break things down into some simple concepts.

One of Oprah Winfrey's lessons from her earlier life is to know that there is always more out there. Just as she did when she was younger, knowing that there is more out there can provide the motivation to do the necessary work until you get where you want to be.

More than motivation, this tip highlights the importance of education. The reason that young Oprah knew about the whole other world that she wanted to reach for was that she read about it. She concentrated on her education. She was able to get out due to that same education, which afforded her a scholarship.

Another important lesson is that obstacles don't deter someone with passion. Winfrey came from a background that many would consider disadvantaged, but these obstacles did not stop her. She says that she could not have done what she did without the advantages of her education.

Finally, do work that you love and that fulfils you. Oprah knew what she wanted from an early age. She pursued her ideals throughout her career and carried them over into her philanthropic work.

Pierre Omidyar

"The Internet is changing everything, and has changed the world in such a short period of time, and will continue to change things in very positive ways that we have yet to anticipate."

Pierre Omidyar

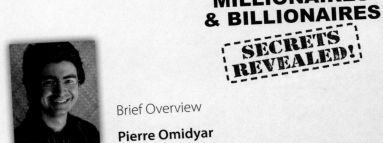

MILLIONAIRES & BILLIONAIRES

SECRETS REVEALED!

Brief Overview

Pierre Omidyar

Born:	21st June, 1967, in Paris
Business:	Founder of the eBay website, Omidyar Network Ink Development Corporation
Industry:	Information Technology and Internet Auctions
Income:	$5.5 billion
Lives:	Honolulu, Hawaii, USA
Family:	Wife, Pam and 3 children
Charities:	Donated $50 million to the Hawaii Community Foundation and also has his own charity network.
Status:	Billionaire

Profile

Pierre Omidyar is the founder of the website eBay. As such, he has been a smashing success in a very short time, and at a young age. He is a guy who was fascinated by computers from a young age. His work and his passion coincided with the explosive advent of the internet for everyday users.

eBay became a cornerstone of internet commerce. The free marketplace of eBay was part of a new economic dimension and made Omidyar a multi-billionaire. He was almost an overnight success and his rise survived the ups and downs of the early online markets.

eBay has taken its place among the giants of the internet. It is a household name and Omidyar is responsible for all of it. The tremendous success of the venture was a combination of fascination with new technology, passion, flexible thinking, and a bit of lucky timing.

Finally, Pierre Omidyar is a philanthropist. He and his wife created the Omidyar Network, which supports and promotes the efforts of organisations that extend help to the poor by increasing and encouraging economic and business opportunities, and by establishing and defending property rights for the poorest people around the world.

Background

Pierre Omidyar was born in Paris, France, on 21 June, 1967. His parents were both from Iran and had been sent to France to study at university. Both his parents were accomplished and high-achieving. His father was a physician and his mother received her advanced degree in linguistics from the Sorbonne.

Pierre's family moved to the US when Pierre was 6 years old. His father had accepted a residency at Johns Hopkins University Medical Center, and so the young Pierre Omidyar grew up mostly in Maryland state, near Washington, D.C. He attended St. Andrew's Episcopal School in nearby Potomac, Maryland, and was interested in computers from a very young age. By the time he reached 9th grade (at the age of 14), Omidyar's passion for computers had solidified. This is when he wrote his first computer program, which put the school library catalogue on to the computer.

Pierre went on to study computer science at Tufts University in Massachusetts. He graduated from Tufts in 1988.

When he left college, his first job was with Claris, a subsidiary of Apple Corp. Here Omidyar helped to develop the program MacDraw. Three years later, in 1991, he became a co-founder of Ink Development Corporation, along with three associates. This was a pen-based computing company, which also had a division for internet shopping, called eShop. The eShop division later sold to Microsoft in 1996.

By 1995, when he was 28 years old, Omidyar was working for General Magic, a start-up company specialising in handheld communications devices. He had also developed a consulting business, called Echo Bay Technology Group. He was living in San Francisco, California, by that time.

It was then that he wrote the code for and launched eBay. This was on the 4th September, 1995, and the original name of the site was AuctionWeb. There is an oft-published and retold story that the idea was launched as a platform for Omidyar's then-girlfriend (now wife), Pamela Wesley. She had a collection of Pez candy dispensers and, over dinner one night, she told Omidyar that she wished that there were some kind of forum that would allow for exchange with like-minded collectors. It is said that this is where Omidyar originally had the idea for an auction website.

This story, however, was created by a public relations manager based on a kernel of truth. In fact, about the time of the site's creation, he and Pam took a vacation in Europe, where she purchased some Pez dispensers. Upon their return to the states, she did begin to trade with her collection on AuctionWeb. After eBay's first public relations person heard this story, she spun the spirit of the tale into a widely-believed myth that eBay had its beginnings in the collectibles. To this day, the corporate headquarters displays a Pez collection in its offices.

But the actual story has more to do with Pierre Omidyar's thinking about marketplaces and community. This thinking characterised all of Omidyar's work from this point forward.

He started AuctionWeb by wondering about what would happen if someone could create a marketplace from a perfectly level playing field. It was an experiment in what might be the perfect marketplace, and he thought that the internet afforded the perfect opportunity for such commerce, where nothing but the market sets the price, and anyone may participate.

The AuctionWeb code was to be placed as a simple page on Omidyar's Echo Bay Technology Group. However, when he went to register this domain name (Echo Bay), he found that the name had already been taken. So, Omidyar abbreviated the site to eBay, and the name was registered.

This is how the auction site was born. At the time, the company was run out of Omidyar's apartment in California. The first item ever sold on eBay was not a Pez dispenser. It was, in fact, a broken laser pointer that went for a winning bid of $14.83, to—what else?—a collector of broken laser pointers! Two years later, in 1997, AuctionWeb underwent the official name change to eBay, and was growing by leaps and bounds. Omidyar had left his day job at General Magic to focus on his growing business full-time.

Today, eBay boasts regular annual revenues averaging $50 billion dollars US per annum. In 2009, eBay saw $8.7 billion in increased sales from 84 million users visiting eBay from every corner of the globe. Its growth into the class of billion-dollar revenue generators was faster even than other major computing giants, including Microsoft itself.

There is almost nothing that has not been bought and sold on eBay. Omidyar's experiment in a level marketplace is a worldwide phenomenon and has changed the way that people think about business. Anyone who can get access to a computer can buy, sell and trade.

Today, Omidyar is 42 and still a young man. He resides in Honolulu, Hawaii, US. He and his wife, Pam, have three children. He now focuses most of his unflagging energy on his philanthropic work. Omidyar is still passionately interested in the interplay of marketplace and community. His eBay experiment left him struck by the power of people to do things if they have a sense of community and a way of doing business. He notes the trust between one stranger and another. He told an interviewer for USA Today that the most significant lesson learned from eBay is "The remarkable fact that 135 million people have learned they can trust a complete stranger. That's had an incredible social impact. People have more in common than they think."

He is now applying the model that he applied to his auction site to the Omidyar Network, his philanthropic organisation that supports nonprofit and for-profit ventures alike. A big part of this project is microfinance. These are very small loans made to poor people so that they can start businesses wherever they are. The eBay model of linking people around the world who are willing to participate has obvious applications for this idea.

What started as an interest in computers grew into a passion for using computing technology to foster a community. The free and open marketplace forum for eBay users became a powerful example of the ability for people to form communities, even when they never meet face to face.

Wealth Creation

Omidyar's story is not exactly a rags-to-riches tale. He was born to well-to-do parents and enjoyed the advantages of a comfortable upbringing and good education. He has, to say the least, made the most of his opportunities.

With the examples of success before him in his parents, Pierre has been able to pursue his passion his whole life. He has done little but play with the technology that fascinated him. "Play" is the word—Omidyar impresses one as a man who simply plays with toys—and has brought it to a lifelong obsession. Underlying the play are serious ideas about how people relate to each other and how the interplay of the market and the idea of community can change things and have an effect on the world.

eBay, or rather AuctionWeb as it was known at first, was successful from the beginning, making Omidyar an overnight success. The short time frame between its launch and its success sometimes obscures the difficulty of pulling off such a venture. Rapid growth causes problems of its own. AuctionWeb had begun in 1995. By 1997, it was growing so rapidly that Omidyar could hardly keep up. He made changes to the form of the site, effectively turning the AuctionWeb site into the eBay company with venture funding.

They searched for a CEO, and scored a coup in the hiring of Meg Whitman. She was able to successfully leave her corporate management style behind in order to adapt to the new mentality of internet commerce. Meg Whitman took the executive helm, although Omidyar remained as chairman of the board. Whitman became the most formidable woman in American business, only surpassed in wealth by Oprah Winfrey in the 2000s. She helped to steer the company to the powerhouse it has become.

When Whitman joined in 1997, the company was mostly just trying to keep up with itself. Usages placed such demand on eBay's servers that the site crashed regularly. These crises peaked in June of 1999, when eBay went down for 22 full hours. The site was completely redone on Whitman's instructions, and she also had every one of eBay's employees (there were 400 by this time) call and personally apologise to 10,000 of eBay's most active users for the mishap. None of these difficulties stopped Omidyar, Whitman or eBay for long.

The company's public financial offering was launched in 1998. Putting the company on the public market made Omidyar a billionaire. This was scarcely three years after AuctionWeb launched. Within the following year, Omidyar was worth nearly $3 billion.

Today, eBay continues to expand, with share prices rising 115% in 2009, doing $8.7 billion in sales. This boosted Omidyar's personal fortune to the recent Forbes estimated net worth of $5.2 billion. Omidyar also returned to his roots in computer communications. He was chairman of Skype until he sold the company in 2009, at an estimated value of $2.75 billion.

Omidyar didn't sit back and luxuriate in his wealth. He remains the chairman of eBay. He lives quite simply, especially for such a wealthy person, although he does have a bodyguard. Overall, he remains a soft-spoken and unassuming person. Far from letting wealth go to his head, he continues to work and to expand his efforts into applying the principles, which he learned during his rise to wealth, to philanthropy.

Pierre Omidyar started with a simple, yet powerful, idea. He wanted to connect people over the internet, providing an even field and access to anyone with an internet connection. He said that he "wanted to give the power of the market back to individuals".

He believes in people. He believes in the power of technology to bring people together. He didn't preach about this idea, he put it into action. Within a few short years, hundreds of millions of users had put their trust into this marketplace and each other, confirming Omidyar's beliefs in an unanswerable fashion.

Traditional, bricks and mortar commerce was never the same again, thanks to Omidyar and a few other intrepid pioneers of the internet. Now, no one has to get a loan, go into debt, purchase inventory, rent a space and launch a business, staking everything on its success. Omidyar had the insight to grasp that the advent of the internet erased the need for sellers and customers to reach each other geographically.

Almost anyone can, and has, used eBay in one way or another. Suddenly, the junk from closets, attics, and curio cabinets were the seeds of a few extra dollars, or an at-home business. Omidyar and the other eBay executives are not the only ones who profited from eBay. The auction site has launched countless other, smaller businesses, allowing people to support themselves entirely by taking advantage of what eBay offers—a platform to sell anything.

Absolutely anything. The site has launched its own little world.

Friends and business partners of ours, Matt and Amanda Clarkson, have created an amazing eBay business, which brings them in passively over $50,000 a month for only 2 hours a week effort as, due to the power of eBay, its now 90% automated. This helped them become multimillionaires which lead them into creating the world's No# 1 eBay education company, which specialises in helping thousands of people around the world use eBay as a way of creating financial freedom.

eBay, as a company, find the right people that have passion, drive and great leadership skills, such as the Australian eBay CEO Deborah Sharkey. While talking to Deborah, she shared with us how Australia's eBay office has out performed the US head office on certain areas within the business.

> "156th richest person in the world."

There are news stories and websites devoted to the strangest items sold on eBay, the highest-priced items sold on eBay, etc. Most people stick to selling pedestrian items such as clothing, sports equipment and furniture. But wild and bizarre items go up for auction too. There was the grilled-cheese sandwich with the image of the Virgin Mary. One man attempted to sell a soul—the soul of one of his friends, who was an atheist, before the auction was shut down. The auction site is actually the largest used auto marketplace in the world, spawning its own division of eBay Motors. People can, and do, sell anything, and big money as well as small money can be made by everyone. Not the least of whom is the site's creator.

Pierre Omidyar is now, by one recent estimate, the 156th richest person in the world. Forbes shows him at number 148 on its list of The World's Billionaires. Most of this vast fortune simply comes directly as a result of eBay. Omidyar is not the type of entrepreneur who has ventured out into a branched network of corporations to make his fortune. He grew one project into one of the single biggest money-makers in history.

Achievements and Foundations

Pierre Omidyar has made major philanthropic contributions since making his fortune. Most notably, the Omidyar Network is a firm intended to catalyse change by making investments in people. True to form, Omidyar wants to do something new in the field of philanthropy, just as he did in the field of business. He is not alone in this. The new billionaires of Silicon Valley created a new movement in the late 1990s. Traditional charities are clunky, cumbersome, operations that the internet gurus correctly saw as well-intentioned but inefficient. They rely on donations, and then this income is greatly eaten up by operating costs such as administration. They also simply provide food or medicine or school supplies, which is often like throwing handfuls of dirt in an attempt to fill a canyon.

The new wealthy businessmen of the internet age were just the people to see that things could be done in a swifter, cleaner, more efficient and self-sustaining way. Omidyar has said, "When you create wealth in a short time, you think about philanthropy as you think about a business. You don't move from saying, 'How can we rationalise an industry?' to 'Where do I sign the big cheque?'"

Pierre and his wife, Pam, were perfectly willing to spend money on causes they believed in. They were not, however, willing to throw it away if nothing would remain to show for it. A new movement, venture philanthropy, came out of a voluntary think tank of internet tycoons, including Omidyar.

The Omidyar Network makes small-scale investments that are intended to have a big impact. The Omidyars want to see that their efforts and their money don't just go to sustain people who cannot sustain themselves. They want to implement the computer age's version of the old adage,

> "Give a man a fish, and he eats for a day. Teach a man to fish, and he eats for a lifetime."

"Give a man a fish, and he eats for a day. Teach a man to fish, and he eats for a lifetime."

A perfect example of this principle is the microloan program set up by the Omidyar Network. This is the philanthropic version of eBay. Anyone willing and able to provide small sums can make a loan to a prospect in an underprivileged part of the world. These loans are used for ventures, for example, planting a crop or starting a tiny business. Sums that people in the developed world might spend in a day are lifelines to people in third-world countries. The program is a success, with incredibly low default rates.

The Omidyar Network also concerns itself with other wide-ranging issues, including leveraging property rights for people in poor countries, and a division that ensures accountability in the US government. The idea behind all of the work is the one that has been behind every one of Omidyar's ventures: community. He wants to ensure that giving to a charity will start a ripple effect, so that the beneficiaries not only become self-sustaining, but can provide education and jobs to others around them.

Omidyar is not only interested in laying out the structure for these organisations. He puts his considerable fortune where his mouth is. He has currently, in the last year, pledged over $900 million to causes. The Omidyars' struggle to find ways to properly conduct charitable activities is probably unfamiliar to most of us and provides a new perspective. The way they see it, they have so much money to give away and no good efficient way to put that money to use. The Omidyar Network continues to search for ways to improve philanthropy projects. He and his wife, following the trend of many of the ultra-rich, have pledged to give away the vast majority of their fortune. They have put years into the effort. Who knew that giving away money could be more difficult than earning it?

> "Who knew that giving away money could be more difficult than earning it?"

But, Omidyar and others like him are onto something. Even their vast fortunes would simply be a drop in the bucket if given away to all of the worthy causes that could use them. Therefore, Omidyar says that he feels a tremendous responsibility to make sure that his money goes to good use.

He has said that his wealth is so vastly greater than his needs, and the needs of his family, and even his heirs. He says that "a small, small piece" of that fortune is more than enough. As for the rest of it, he doesn't want "to see it go to waste". It is odd in some ways that the overnight success stories seem to have much greater insight than the old-money guard of charitable causes, who are used to donating money for philanthropic purposes.

On the other hand, the mentality that can write computer code has a gift for seeing things in simple and bare terms. They simply want their money to go to good use, instead of being poured down a sinkhole.

The Omidyar Network is only one of the causes that Omidyar puts his money into. He donates to many other worldwide causes, as well as US ones. Pierre and his wife have pledged to give away 99% of their vast fortune over 20 years. It will take Omidyar many times longer to give his money away than it did for him to earn it in the first place.

Omidyar's motivation is not simply the idea of community, although that is the driving force. He and his wife simply do not have the goal of living a lavish lifestyle. He is a producer of products, not a spender of money. He and Pam even worry about the effects of the money on their children.

Aside from his charity work, Pierre Omidyar also has joined the Board of Trustees of Tufts University, his alma mater.

Still, Omidyar's biggest achievement to date remains eBay. The network was an experiment designed by Omidyar. He wanted to see what would happen to a market, if it started with a completely level playing field. The internet was that completely new, open field. As we can all infer, this marketplace took off to dizzying heights. The open commerce of eBay is a place where anyone and everyone can and does come to buy and sell, on a large or small scale.

Pierre Omidyar's Tips for Success

- Pierre once said, "I never had it in mind that I would start a company one day and it would really be successful. I have just been motivated by working on interesting technology." We can see from this that having an all-consuming interest in a particular field is really the seed of the entrepreneurial spirit. Further evidence of this is always to be found in the stories of the successful.

- In the same vein, Omidyar says, "You should pursue your passion. If you're passionate about something and you work hard, then I think you'll be successful. If you start a business because you think you're going to make a lot of money at it,

> "It's all about passion, implemented by means of hard work."

then you probably won't be successful, because that's the wrong reason to start a business. You have to really believe in what you're doing, be passionate enough about it so that you will put in the hours and hard work that it takes to actually succeed there, and then you'll be successful."

Take note of the way that the world's greatest successes tend to give the same, deceptively simple advice. It's all about passion, implemented by means of hard work. Omidyar's story exemplifies this idea. His career begins and continues with the idea of working on a particular interest and developing it into something that works on a new level. Having done this, other people can then utilise it and there is the market.

- Pierre also has a unique insight into the workings of big achievements: "When you look at the accomplishments of accomplished people and you say, 'Boy, that

> "So just go and do it, try it, learn from it."

must have been really hard,' you know, when you look at something that looks hard, that was probably easy. And conversely, when you look at something that looks easy, that was probably hard. And so you're never going to know which is which until you actually go and do it. So just go and do it, try it, learn from it. You'll fail at some things, that's a learning experience that you need so that you can take that on to the next experience. And don't let people who you may respect and who you believe know what they're talking about, don't let them tell you it can't be done, because often they will tell you it can't be done, and it's just because they don't have the courage to try."

Omidyar knows that he is the only one who has done what he did. And he knows that the reason that he has succeeded is that he pioneered his own route to success. He has learned from experience how to do his work, and he can't take other peoples' advice, because no one in the world has any knowledge of how to do the job that he has done.

- Very characteristically, what Omidyar says about the success of eBay is that "the real value and the real power at eBay is the community. It's the buyers and sellers coming together and forming a marketplace." Omidyar is very aware, all the time, of what drives the marketplace. Even in the context of giving away his fortune, he talks about how it was built on the small exchanges of common people. Again, "One of the things that I repeat probably every day here is that our success is built on our community's success."

- Pierre combined people and the internet in a new way. Although it is now an example of social interactions, he says, "When I started eBay, it was a hobby, an experiment to see if people could use the internet to be empowered through access to an efficient market. I actually wasn't thinking about it in terms of a social impact. It was really about helping people connect around a sphere of interest so they could do business." There is big money in facilitating business. And big money in finding your niche where no one realised that a demand existed previously.

- Pierre Omidyar's business success was founded, not so much on trying to outdo the competition in an existing market, but in keeping his organisation a dynamic, ever-changing entity that responded directly to customer needs. He had practically created his own market, and customer feedback was all he had. He described this approach in the interview.

"It was of necessity, frankly...I didn't have a whole plan for how it would evolve. How it did evolve was that users would write to me and say, 'You should do this, you should think about this, you should deal with these issues.' I had the very luxurious job of saying, 'That's a good idea, and that's a good idea, and let me go do that.'"

"It was letting the users take responsibility for building the community." This takes customer service approaches to new heights. eBay was exquisitely responsive to its user base and its popularity soared accordingly.

- Over and over, one can see that Omidyar built his fortune on a certainty that people can make things happen, given the slightest chance. He based his company on it. He says that eBay's basic premises are as follows:

"We believe people are basically good; we believe everyone has something to contribute; we believe that an honest, open environment can bring out the best in people; we recognise and respect everyone as a unique individual; we encourage you to treat others the way you want to be treated. I founded the company on the notion that people were basically good and that if you give them the benefit of the doubt you're rarely disappointed."

So much for the idea that nice guys finish last. Perhaps this is the real key to success. What holds many people back is the fact that they feel they need to protect

> "...fortunes to be made by eBay users."

themselves from hypothetical people who are out to get them. Omidyar seems lacking in the intense mistrust of an open market. Most people think of his basic idea as essentially a dog-eat-dog arena, where unscrupulous people would take advantage of helpless victims, and where the evil lure of profit would ruin morals and lives. eBay provides powerful evidence to the contrary. Omidyar based his whole company on the idea that this openness and ability to interact was, in fact, a central and driving force for good. This simple, yet elusive, idea allowed smaller fortunes to be made by eBay users even as Omidyar amassed his large one.

Summary

Pierre Omidyar's straight-arrow rise provides a very clear and linear example to see. So, let's look at Omidyar's successes and the principles behind them. Success is never easy for anyone. However, looking at Pierre's story, and considering the way he speaks, we can get the feel of a certain ease and a natural feel to the trajectory that his career has taken.

There is some element of luck in this story. After all, Omidyar's interest from an early age in what turned out to be the "next big thing" laid the foundation for the explosive growth that only a new market can provide. However, it is a big mistake to attribute Omidyar's success to luck and timing. After all, he was interested in exciting new technology, and worked on it as a hobby, for reasons that he chose.

Work and persistence pay off no matter what. It doesn't take a crystal ball to follow your enthusiasm and turn it into something that will pay off in a big way. Passion is key. Omidyar simply kept playing around with the technology that he loved, until he found solutions to problems other people had not even conceived.

His example shows that passion, hard work and good essential values, when pursued consistently and tirelessly, lead to great success.

Bill Gates

"It's fine to celebrate success but it is more important to heed the lessons of failure."

Bill Gates

MILLIONAIRES & BILLIONAIRES

SECRETS REVEALED!

Brief Overview

Bill Gates

Born: 29th October, 1955, in Seattle, Washington, USA

Business: Founder of Microsoft

Industry: IT/Software

Income: Net worth $53 billion

Lives: Medina, Washington, USA

Family: Wife, Melinda and 3 children, Jennifer, Phoebe & Rory

Charities: Bill & Melinda Gates Foundation, which has donated over $28 billion to charity so far

Status: Billionaire

Bill Gates

Profile

Plenty of people talk about changing the world. Bill Gates has actually done it. His inventions, and later, his philanthropic activities, have reached into every corner of the globe. We are living in a very different sort of world from only a few decades ago.

The Microsoft founder is almost single-handedly responsible for the PC revolution that has ushered in a new age of communication, commerce, information and media. The ripple effect of Gates' tech tinkering is now incalculable.

Gates was the world's richest man for many years running. The productive power and wealth generated by Bill Gates and his technology is mind-boggling, and he has the profits to prove it. He is using those profits, and the power of his name, to effect other changes. He has now started a huge foundation for charitable purposes, and he continues to expand his repertoire of projects.

When Gates was a young man at Harvard, he was already a master of the very young technology of computers. In the early 1970s, computers were large, enigmatic machines that, as far as most people were concerned, had a place in science fiction and in large, secret, government laboratories. Gates saw things differently, since he was interested in the small, personal computers. He was fascinated by the language of machines and began writing programs for computers that could sit on a person's desk. From that early tinkering, a revolution the likes of which the world has never seen was born.

Background

William H. Gates III had a comfortable start in life. He was born on 28th October, 1955, in Seattle, Washington, USA. His father was an attorney and his mother was a teacher and a businesswoman, involved in the boards of directors of organisations such as the University of Washington, various banks and the United Way. Gates' parents exposed their children from a very early age to the dealings of the outside world, since they were connected to business and government both professionally and socially. Gates was interested in business from a young age and paid attention to these influences.

Bill Gates originally was educated in the typical US public school. He says that the rather slack curriculum and casual student attitudes reinforced more goofing around than it did serious study. Young Gates looked at the manner of school reports that gave separate marks for effort and performance. His goal was to try to have the highest marks in performance, with the least effort, and his grades suffered somewhat.

His parents, who thought that the boy was clever and talented, but failing to apply himself, sent him to the exclusive secondary school, Lakeside School, when he was 12 years old. Although the school later allowed girls and relaxed their strict requirements for uniforms and addressing teachers as "Master", when Gates started, it was a strict boys' school. While Gates was unhappy with the change at first, he soon adjusted to the stronger emphasis on academic performance. Not surprisingly, his strongest talents were in maths and science. The young man settled into a serious course of study, and performed well.

It was here, at Lakeside School, that the course of Gates' life was set. Although computers at that time (during the late 1960s) were hardly a facet of everyday life, the school purchased a single computer and allowed the students to have the use of it. The computer was actually bought and donated after a fundraiser from the Mother's Club, along with some purchase of limited time to hook the phone to the machine and run programs. When Gates speaks of working with computers starting at the age of 12, he makes it sound perfectly natural. In fact, it was an extraordinary situation and an extraordinary opportunity.

From his first exposure to this now-primitive machine, Gates was hooked. It was also here that he met Paul Allen, who soon became his collaborator and business partner, even while they were still schoolboys. The boys, at this time, were fascinated with the new technology, and were among a handful of students that showed determination and an aptitude for using the computer. One gets the distinct impression that Gates knew from the beginning that computers were an important new technology that would have a major impact during the years to come. On the other hand, there were two strange parallel lines of thought in his head at the time, which lasted through his first years at university. As much time as Gates spent working on the computer, and in fact, doing work for computer companies at this time, he had no serious intention of making this his career. It was simply something he was working on in the mean time, until he got through college and started a "regular career".

Gates, Allen and a couple of other students quickly became the nucleus of the computer team at Lakeside. They learned the programming language BASIC and wrote new code for the school system. Their understanding of the GE time-shared machine (so-called due to the fact that the system used a single phone line, and every usage cost money both for time and for individual programs run on it, so that it had to be shared among all users) soon outstripped that of any of the faculty. Gates had read ahead in some of his classes, particularly maths, and was excused from some of his class time in order to focus on computing. Gates and his friends would write code onto yellow tape, and this teletype would then be fed into the machine, so that they wouldn't need to use more time than necessary typing the programs in on the time-shared system.

Gates has told the story that, "The amount of time we'd spend in this particular room that had the Teletype was quite extreme. We sort of took over the room, myself and two other people. They called it the 'Teletype Room'." Gates' first program was one that would allow a user to play tic-tac-toe against the computer.

Gates and his friends were interested in not only computers, but business, even during these early teen years. As Gates warmed to his new school environment, he explains, "I did eventually find some friends there, some of who [sic] had the same sort of interests, like reading business magazines and Fortune. We were always creating funny company names and having people send us their product literature. Trying to think about how business worked. And in particular, looking at computer companies and what was going on with them."

The boys quickly ran through the school's budget that allowed them access to the computer time. They began constantly scheming for ways and means to get more access. They talked companies into loaning machines to the school, in return for work. They convinced a local company to loan them a computer. This company had a deal with the parent computer company, DEC-10, that if they could find problems with the computer, they could use it rent-free. Eventually the boys' debugging efforts, coupled with the fact that they had actually hacked into company personnel information, got them into hot water.

Gates and his friends continued to find other computers. They would go down to the Computer Center Corporation (known locally as C-Cubed), to borrow computer time there. They would dig through the garbage, looking for code tape, and study the code to look for mistakes and see what they could learn. By then,

Gates, Allen and two other friends had formed a tight group that called itself the Lakeside Programming Group. "We were the hard-core users," says Gates. This enabled Gates to learn other computer languages.

Gates was still a boy at Lakeside when he landed his first programming jobs. The Lakeside Programming Group wrote a complex program to help the school with its scheduling system, and received payment for it. The boys contacted an Oregon company that hired them to write a payroll program. Gates, who along with one friend, was two years younger than the other two, was initially kicked off of this project by his peers when they thought that there was not enough work. However, the program turned out to be far more complex than they originally thought, and they asked Gates to rejoin. Gates had the temerity to tell them, "Look, if you want me to come back you have to let me be in charge. But this is a dangerous thing, because if you put me in charge this time, I'm going to want to be in charge forever after." The program got done, and, although they did not know it at the time, the basic structure of the future Microsoft was set.

Gates even worked processing data to monitor traffic, and for TRW, the office that managed the power grid for the Pacific Northwest. He took off part of his senior year and wrote programs for the power industry at TRW. This seems like heady stuff, but Gates still had not decided on computers as a career.

In 1973, Gates began attending Harvard University. His friend Paul Allen, who was two years older and had been attending the University of Washington, got a job at Honeywell in nearby Boston, so the two continued to spend time together, working on the programming language BASIC and talking computer technology. Bill was studying math, still with the idea of a "regular career". However, he and Allen at this time continued to come up with new ideas for computing, and Allen brought to Gates' notice of the new microchip processor technology, showing him a magazine article on the subject. Very early, Gates and Allen talked about a day when there would be a computer "on every desk and in every home".

In those days, the computers still cost tens of thousands of dollars. One day in 1973, Gates and Allen were walking in Harvard Square, and noticed the latest issue of Popular Electronics. The cover story described a new computer kit—small and inexpensive. The new Altair 8800 had been developed and was on the market from MITS in Albuquerque, New Mexico. The machine really could do very little; it was strictly hardware.

Gates and Allen knew that they could write BASIC software for the new machine. The fact that the microcomputer, that they had predicted was coming, was now on the market gave them a sense of urgency. They worried that the advances were happening without them. So, they contacted MITS by letter immediately, offering to write a version of BASIC to run on the Altair. MITS was sceptical, and was receiving many proposals, but told the young men to go ahead and give it a try.

The problem was that they did not have an Altair of their own to work on. Allen wrote a program to simulate the machine, based on pictures and the magazine article description. Both Gates and Allen then worked day and night to write the software. Six weeks later, they had it done, and Allen flew out to Albuquerque with the program written on Teletype tape. In spite of the difficulties, the program worked without a single bug, and MITS decided to purchase the program.

The technical genius of Gates and Allen had produced the first software in existence for inexpensive personal computing. The business genius in Gates now came into play. They demanded a licence, and an agreement from MITS to allow them to sell the software to other companies, as well.

Gates decided that this venture now had a good chance of succeeding and decided to drop out of Harvard to pursue the work in partnership with Allen. Gates and Allen moved to Albuquerque early in 1975 to devote themselves to business. Bill Gates was 19 years old. Gates and Allen made their new business partnership official, registering the company name as Micro-soft, which is short for microcomputer software.

Micro-soft continued to develop software for MITS, and also produced programs for other companies. The work was almost unbelievably demanding on the small staff of a few people and no one worked harder than Gates. He often worked day and night. Over the next four years, the fledgling company programmed, and hired new people when they could. While building Micro-soft, Gates began a fierce and early fight against software piracy. At first, the internet was considered a free-for-all of information sharing and it was often treated as though no one owned the software. Gates understood that intellectual production in the intangible world of the information superhighway is nonetheless property and began to defend it. He wrote his famous "Letter to Hobbyists", explaining that the work was copyrighted and needed to be paid for. When people pirated the software, Micro-soft struggled to meet payroll. Gates explained that they needed to get paid so that they could continue to write more programs.

> "Gates was 19 years old. Gates and Allen made their new business partnership official, registering the company name as Micro-soft."

> "He often worked day and night."

Several years after the move to Albuquerque, MITS was sold to another company. This company relocated to California. Since the relative remoteness of Albuquerque made it difficult to recruit the highly intelligent and specialised minds needed at what was now Microsoft (with the hyphen having been dropped), Gates and Allen decided to relocate, too. Microsoft now had about sixteen people. All but one of them made the move back to Washington. Microsoft was now established in Bellevue, Washington, near Gates' Seattle birthplace. The move happened in 1979, four years after the company was established. In 1986, the company moved to a new location one more time, but only a short distance away. The new location, in Redmond, Washington, is still the location of the vast Microsoft campus.

Microsoft was on the rise, but the move that really sealed the company's success was the decision of giant IBM to launch a PC. They turned to Microsoft to write the software and help design the system.   The software that resulted was Microsoft Disk Operating System, or MS-DOS. Bill Gates, as he had always done, insisted on the right to license the software to other companies. IBM's computer was a huge seller. Although Microsoft did not make royalties off of all of the sales, having licensed DOS to IBM for a flat fee, competing companies could do best by licensing Microsoft's software for their own products.   Not only did Microsoft have a major product with the IBM product, but they were able to license the software to other companies, who could sell their computers as "IBM-compatible" systems. Gates' success was assured.

In 1983, the legendarily close and successful partnership of Bill Gates and Paul Allen ended. Although they remained close friends, Allen left Microsoft after developing Hodgkin's disease. When Allen retired, he himself was the world's fourth-richest man. In 2010, Allen pledged to leave his own enormous fortune to Gates' philanthropic foundation, which will be described in a later section.

In 1985, Microsoft introduced Windows. This graphic interface was the big introduction that could compete with the other big seller, Apple's Macintosh (which Gates had actually helped to develop earlier). The foundation programs of DOS and Windows were run on the vast majority of personal computers on earth.

Ten years after the introduction of Windows (in 1995), Bill Gates was the richest man on earth. His systems, which run the company cornerstone applications of Office, Power Point and Internet Explorer, allow the world to work, play and connect with each other in a way that is utterly novel in human history.

> "In 1995, Bill Gates was the richest man on earth."

Bill Gates married in 1994. His wife, Melinda, was an employee of Microsoft when she caught Bill's eye at a seminar. The couple have three children.

Gates finally stepped down from the CEO position of Microsoft in the year 2000, although he retains the Board of Directors chair. He now spends much of his time working on the Bill and Melinda Gates Foundation, the philanthropic organisation set up at the suggestion of Gates' father.

Wealth Creation

Gates achieved success at an early age with Microsoft. He managed to make himself an overnight success in the field before he graduated from university. His operating system, MS-DOS, allowed IBM, Hewlett-Packard and other computing giants to make inroads into the new personal computing market.

When Gates was only 17, he was getting paid for writing programming language. The payroll program that he and the rest of his cronies at Lakeside wrote for the Oregon company paid over $4,000. This is a lot of money for a high-school student today, and that was in 1972. Even the Lakeside School paid the group for programs. So Gates was making money practically from the start.

Gates was a man (or boy) of business from a very young age. He learned about payroll, taxes and regulations, working on that early payroll program. Through his parents' connections, he came under the influence of businesspeople and government people as a child. He read up on business models and styles at Lakeside.

He and Allen had their own business, Traf-O-Data, with their traffic-monitoring program, also when he was at secondary school. So, by the time Microsoft was founded, Gates, at 19, was already an experienced man of business. His foresight into the idea of licensing software to multiple companies, rather than selling each program to a single company, was really what made Microsoft the success that it became.

Very early on, Gates understood another key point, especially in the high-tech, cutting-edge world that he worked in. He was adamant about having stringent standards for hiring smart people. His hiring practices were ruthless. He wanted only the best. He got it, too, and he sought for unusual minds.

Unlike many entrepreneurs, Gates did not gamble everything in the beginning. Some people eventually make it big by getting in over their heads with debts and investments, staking it all on success. Gates' approach was far more meticulous and careful.

An interview with Gates reveals how he managed to have huge goals, but build the early business by starting on a small scale: "Even in the early days, if you set a computer on every desk in every home, and you'd say, 'Okay, how many homes are there in the world? How many desks are there in the world? Can I make $20.00 for every home, $20.00 for every desk?' You could get these big numbers. But part of the beauty of the whole thing was we were very focused on the here and now. Should we hire one more person? If our customers didn't pay us, would we have enough cash to meet the payroll? We really were very practical about that next thing, and so involved in the deep engineering

> "He was now 31 years old, and the youngest billionaire in history."

that we didn't get ahead of ourselves. We never thought how big we'd be. I remember when one of the early lists of wealthy people came out and one of the Intel founders was there, the guy that ran Wang computers... and we thought, 'Hmm. Boy, if the software business does well, the value of Microsoft could be similar to that.' But it wasn't a real focus. The everyday activity of just doing great software drew us in. And some decisions we made—like the quality of the people, the way we were very global, the vision of how we thought about software—that was very long term. But other than those things, we just came into work every day and wrote more code and hired more people. It wasn't really until the IBM PC succeeded, and perhaps even until Windows succeeded, that there was a broad awareness that Microsoft was...unique as a software company, and that these other companies had been one-product companies, hadn't hired people, couldn't do a broad set of things, didn't renew their excellence, didn't do research. So we thought we were doing something very unique, but it was easily not until 1995, or even 1997, that there was this wide recognition that we were the company that had revolutionised software."

Even if it wasn't widely recognised at first, Gates was building an enormous fortune. In 1978, when Microsoft was still in Albuquerque, New Mexico, the company's sales for the year passed the one million dollar mark. In 1986, shortly after the move from Bellevue to Redmond, Microsoft made a public stock offering. The next year, after taking Microsoft public, Gates was worth one billion dollars. He was now 31 years old, and the youngest billionaire in history.

By the time that Gates mentions that his company gained its widespread recognition, in 1995, Gates reached the position of the world's richest man, with a net worth of $18.5 billion. Gates was only 40 years old at the time. The next year, although his net worth had doubled, he was No#2. In 1998, Gates reached number one again on the list of the richest on earth. He held this position for ten full years. In 2008, he was finally back at number 2, second to his friend, Warren Buffett. The very next year, he was back at number one. He has slipped again, but the 53 year-old Gates is still sitting pretty.

The kernel of the burgeoning of success for Gates was obviously his early fascination with new technology, coupled with an intrepid foray into business practices without worrying about the fact that he was considered too young to be in business. The rest is due to his aggressive business practices, and his insistence on building a company that had very different hiring practices than the rest of the corporate world. Microsoft hired untried, untested, people who were smart and eager.

Gates says of the early days of the company, "Our hiring was always focused on people right out of school. We had a few key hires...who came in with experience. But most of our developers, we decided that we wanted them to come with clear minds, not polluted by some other approach, to learn the way that we liked to develop software, and to put the kind of energy into it that we thought was key." He also focused on building small teams, putting them in control, and giving them the best possible tools for the job.

Gates saw an early possibility and how to bring it to fruition. He built his fortune on the world telecommunication and information revolution, and helped to make that revolution happen. Microsoft built the world's biggest share of wealth. This wealth did not only belong to Gates, but to his early associates, all of whom became billionaires. At last count, Bill Gates' net worth was estimated at $53 billion.

Achievements and Foundations

The achievements of Bill Gates can hardly be overestimated. He helped to create a new world of information and access to information and technology that is now available to common working people. He continues to try to make this technology available to people in highly underprivileged parts of the world. Gates has donated a great deal of money. Bill and his wife,

> "The Bill and Melinda Gates Foundation has endowments of over $28 billion US."

Melinda, have made it their goal to give away the majority of their vast fortune. Education is a big priority—they have given large amounts to schools and libraries. Recently, Gates began a gradual process of stepping back from Microsoft to part-time work, as Chairman of the Board and Chief Software Architect, so that he could devote more serious time to working on a new project—his charitable foundation.

Bill Gates is the creator of one of the world's largest charitable foundations. The Bill and Melinda Gates Foundation has endowments of over $28 billion US. The foundation receives over $1 billion US in annual donations. Even Warren Buffett, who will be included later in this book, pledged the majority of his fortune to the foundation.

Gates is making a serious project of the foundation, treating it like a job, and devoting the same serious attention to it that he did to his position at Microsoft. Gates says, "The Foundation got started in the late 90s, with my dad encouraging me.... I was still very busy, our kids were very young, but we got going. We put computers in libraries in many different countries, including the United States. We did some scholarship things. We were learning about reproductive health and population issues. And that kept growing and we met people who knew about vaccines. So it was a part-time thing. Global health was a bit over half; the US focused libraries, scholarship education work was over a quarter; and it was a final piece that relates to other things to help the poorest, other than just health things, things like finance and savings. And you know, it grew. And then I saw that I could make a unique contribution there, and created a transition plan that was four years in the making. So now I'm full time at the Foundation and playing a role of being the Chairman and travelling a lot. So it's equally challenging; it's very fulfilling. It's taking these resources that I'm lucky enough to have because of the success of Microsoft and giving those back to the society in a way that can have the biggest impact."

The Bill and Melinda Gates Foundation does not merely deliver computers and money to organisations. They focus on research, just like Gates always did at Microsoft.

"We need new vaccines, we need cheap vaccines, we need vaccines that are easy to deliver, even in the poorest places, where something like having refrigerators is tough to do. And it does connect to my experience at Microsoft of finding great scientists, making sure they understand the problems that are important, getting them focused on those things, having milestones, even if there are setbacks, and making sure that...they get the proper backing. This is something that governments don't do much of. They fund a lot of the great delivery—the foreign aid is very, very important—but on the discovery side there's been a deep under-investment. Whether it's a malaria vaccine, tuberculosis vaccine, about 20 different diseases that, if things go well, we'll have vaccines for most of those within the next decade. So the Foundation is really taking the lead, financing scientific work, and already some have been discovered. Some are getting out there, but there's a lot more still to be done."

Gates is probably the man to do it. There is no doubt that he can get things done.

Gates received an honorary KBE in 2005 for services in reducing poverty and improving health in developing countries.

In 2009, Gates was recognised with the Indira Ghandi Prize for Peace, Disarmament and Development. This prize was awarded by the president of India. Gates' Foundation has pledged almost a billion dollars in India alone. In that country, most of the donations have gone toward trying to end polio and for AIDS prevention efforts.

Although Gates never returned to study at Harvard, after dropping out in 1975 to head to Albuquerque and form his company, he did finally get his Harvard degree. In 2007, Bill Gates was asked to speak at the commencement ceremony at Harvard University. While there, he was awarded an honorary doctor of law degree. Gates finally received his degree 32 years after dropping out. He also received an honorary degree from Cambridge University in 2009. He and his wife were both made doctors of law for their work as heads of the Bill and Melinda Gates Foundation.

Bill Gates has published two books. The first was published in 1995, the year that Gates became the wealthiest man on earth. The book was *The Road Ahead*. The work describes his future vision for digital technology. It became a bestseller. The second book, *Business @ the Speed of Thought*, also rose to the top of the bestseller list. This book describes the ways in which technology and business are inextricably linked.

Gates can be credited, without exaggeration, with helping to change the world. Information, entertainment, communication, and work alike are at the fingertips of billions of people, who can call up any sort of tool, fact, game, film, or research at the press of a few keys, or with the click of a button. Bill Gates and his contemporaries started a revolution, and society has not looked the same since. Paper is, in many ways, now antiquated.

Work, play, even philanthropy, are all done differently now. The slim, impossibly young, geeky, book smart, math student—along with his friends, colleagues, associates, and contemporaries in the field, made nerdiness cool and showed us all a new way of doing things.

Bill Gates' Tips for Success

- Gates credits his upbringing with starting him off right. He says that his parents pushed him to do things that he wasn't particularly good at or comfortable with. From this he learned to tackle anything he set his mind to and not to be confined by his past track record or his own particular bent.

  "My mom and dad were great at encouraging me as a kid to do things that I wasn't good at, to go out for a lot of different sports. At the time, I thought it was kind of pointless, but it ended up really exposing me to leadership opportunities and showing me that I wasn't good at a lot of things, instead of sticking to things that I was comfortable with. It was fantastic, and now some of those activities I cherish. They had to stick to it, because I pushed back a lot, but it was fantastic advice."

- Gates also advises on the importance of keeping things simple. As with other astounding success stories, he follows simple principles with focused intensity. He thinks in simple terms—probably being used to thinking in the language of programming helps with this mindset.

- Gates is a man who also mentions kindness in the context of success. A close friend and admirer of Warren Buffett, Gates was struck by the unassuming kindness of another of the world's most successful men. "I think Warren is so nice to everybody – how does he say no in a nice way? He turns down an unbelievable number of things and yet everybody feels great about it. His grace in talking to people... I do find myself thinking, hmm, *how would Warren say this in a friendly fashion*?"

- Gates has an interesting take on his work, too. He accepted feedback on the quality of his products, most notably from Japan. He can accept tough criticism and only pushes to make things better. "Our Japanese customers on the whole were so tough about quality and precision – that was fantastic, because we did a lot of business there early in our existence."

> "The ability to accept, rather than to avoid, criticism is crucial to continuing development."

The ability to accept, rather than to avoid, criticism is crucial to continuing development. Even as a young teenager, a famously defensive age, Gates welcomed criticism. A programmer at C-Cubed used to take Gates' computer code, and "tear it apart", which Gates thought was an amazing way to learn to be an excellent programmer.

> "Genius is one percent inspiration and 99 percent perspiration."

- Gates says that, in the long run, hard work is far more important than intelligence when it comes to success. He says that it is a result of "dedication and persistence" rather than "brilliance". He believes in the quote that "Genius is one percent inspiration and 99 percent perspiration." Hard work is certainly part of Gates' life. He has worked long, tireless hours making Microsoft what it is. He demands the same of those who work for him.

- Gates says that he is "acutely conscious of the value of time." He doesn't waste a moment. He spent most of his days in meetings, and kept them all business. He makes the most of every second. He works tirelessly, and he is always doing something. Making every second count, it's not hard to imagine why Gates became the world's youngest billionaire. He did not wait until he was through even with secondary school to start working at night, almost every night, on computing.

- He also says that keeping an eye on the competition is crucial. He has always put this into practice. He studies what's happening in the field all the time. Rather than looking for weaknesses in his competitors that he can exploit, he seeks out their strengths. He does not want to plume himself by comparing what he does well to what others do poorly. He wants to seek out real threats, so that he can keep Microsoft in a competitive position.

- Bill Gates insists, along with others, that all successful people have vision. He knows that vision means being able to see clearly what one wants, and to see things that don't exist today, but that can be created.

> "...all successful people have vision."

Very early on, Gates and Allen had a vision of the time when there would be "a computer on every desk and in every home". They could see the possibility clearly, despite the fact that even people in the industry at the time could not. Gates says, "At the time, you have people who are very smart saying, 'Why would somebody need a computer?' Even Ken Olsen, who had run this company Digital Equipment, who made the computer I grew up with, and that we admired both him and his company immensely, was saying that this seemed kind of a silly idea that people would want to have a computer."

Today, it is hard to imagine what life would be like without computers. Before Gates and his cronies, people could not imagine life with computers. That is vision—it was unimaginable to most a little over 30 years ago, but a select few had the vision to not only imagine it, but to make it happen.

Even for the vast majority of people, whose work will always be on a much smaller scale, vision is the key to success. No one can achieve a goal without knowing what that goal is. No one can set goals without being able to imagine some possibilities. When a person can see what's possible in a clear enough way to break it down into a goal and a plan for reaching it, then that person has vision.

- Although Gates is the world's most successful college dropout, he does not underestimate the value of education. He says that the only reason that he left Harvard is that the timing of the fast-moving industry was so important that he couldn't afford to wait to complete his studies. However, he still says that "There is nothing better than a great college for your experience. I would have stayed until the end if it hadn't been for the urgency. I watch lots of college lectures online now because I enjoy that so much. So unless you have something that's really uniquely, amazingly time dependent, it's a great thing to finish the degree."

- Finally, Gates says that "fanaticism is underrated", and he is not a man of moderation. "I think fanaticism is underrated. I'm a fanatic about running the engineering groups and the quality of them. Steve [Jobs] is a fanatic about the user experience and the design, and it clearly has made a huge difference for Apple."

This is an important point. Gates is such a success because he demands excellence from himself and his products. He did not build his empire by lacking the perfectionist tendency. He did not become a success by doing enough work to get by. He did not become the world's wealthiest man by living with what was good enough. He demanded the utmost of effort and excellence, from himself and others. He was fanatically devoted to building Microsoft, and to making it a leader. He succeeded beyond the wildest dreams of anyone. Anyone, that is, except Bill Gates.

Summary

Bill Gates is a larger-than-life example. What can we take from his story?

One lesson is about the perfection of single-minded enthusiasm. Bill Gates spent time messing around with computers before he became rich. He was simply interested and he never stopped.

In addition, Gates was in the vanguard of the "nerd" revolution. Before "geek chic" was cool, Gates was simply going with his area of interest. He pursued what was then an obscure project, because he had found his passion. We all know how well this paid off by now.

Finally, Gates is an example of persistence in the face of all opposition. Early success did not stop him from facing many obstacles.

He has been in and out of courtrooms for most of his professional life, branded as a monopolist in the field that he was largely responsible for creating, and under whose example and using whose products a whole host of other, competing companies are thriving. Gates has been a fierce businessman and a tough defender of his own products in a world that often condemns and vilifies him for it.

Gates' success is stellar and he is a prime example of the billionaire mindset.

Warren Buffett

*"It's better to hang out with people better than you.
Pick out associates whose behavior is better than
yours and you'll drift in that direction."*

Warren Buffett

Brief Overview

Warren Buffett

Born:	30th August, 1930, in Omaha, Nebraska, USA
Business:	Chairman & CEO of Berkshire Hathaway
Industry:	Share Market Investor
Income:	Net worth $47 billion
Lives:	Omaha, Nebraska, USA
Family:	Wife, Astrid, and 3 children, Susan, Howard and Peter
Charities:	Susan Thompson Buffett Foundation and contributes to many others
Status:	Billionaire

Warren Buffett

Profile

Warren Buffett is the undisputed king of investing. The unassuming-looking man from a Midwestern US state might be the last person that you would identify as a powerhouse in the dizzying, gilded, excess-laden echelon of the super-wealthy. But if you guessed that this rather plain man was just another Midwestern, down-home, good-hearted man living a simple life, you would be both right and very wrong.

> "He has traded places with Bill Gates as the world's richest man."

The simple man from Nebraska is also one of the world's wealthiest men. He has traded places with Bill Gates as the world's richest man. His business acumen is legendary. He has a talent for picking investments that would give a person the impression that he has found a way to foretell the future.

Warren Buffett seems to have had a penchant for doing business almost since the day he was born. He started as a small-time entrepreneur in his teens, working tirelessly on one venture or another.

By the time he had graduated from college, he had accumulated a savings account that many people might envy after a lifetime of work. By his early 30s, Buffett was a millionaire. By the time most people consider retiring, he was a billionaire. Warren

Buffett's investment strategy made him a huge success, and he is now sought after as a guru by anyone seeking advice on making money.

Background

On 30 August, 1930, Warren Edward Buffett was born in Omaha, Nebraska, USA. He was the second child of parents Howard Buffett, a stockbroker, and Leila, a housewife. Even as a young child, Warren had a head for business and a head for figures. He was able to add up long columns of figures in his head.

"Buffet's first investment lost money almost immediately."

When Warren was 6 years old, he began his first business venture. His grandfather owned a local grocery store. He would purchase Coca Cola in 6-packs from the store for twenty-five cents each. He would then go out and sell each bottle for five cents, clearing a profit of five cents per 6-pack. He also sold chewing gum and magazines. Buffett was already earning his own money in post-depression era America, when many were still struggling. He worked in the grocery store to earn extra cash in addition to his entrepreneurial activities, all while still attending Rose Hill Elementary School.

The child who would later become rich from the stock market made his first business investment at the age of 11. He decided to purchase three shares of Cities Service Preferred at the price of $38 per share, on behalf of himself and his older sister, Doris. Buffett's first investment lost money almost immediately. The share price dropped to $27 per share following Warren's purchase. The boy was frightened by this, but had the sense to hold onto the stock until it rebounded. When the Cities Service shares rose again, Buffett sold them for $40 per share, making a small profit. He continued to follow their performance, watching in dismay as the shares then rocketed to a value of $200 each. Buffett had lost out on a small fortune. He says that was his first lesson in the value of patience in investing.

This is a lesson that many people never manage to implement. Warren Buffett was still a child when he learned a lesson that would pay off big in the years to come.

The initial investment followed a trip to New York that Buffett had taken with his family. At the age of 10, young Warren Buffett made a point of visiting, amid all of the attractions of a major city for a child of the Midwest Great Plains, the New York Stock Exchange. The exchange must have been a wonderland to the young man, but it was not his first exposure to investing.

His stockbroker father had a local firm in Omaha and Buffett used to spend time in the customer's lounge of another brokerage near his father's office.

> "He delivered newspapers, detailed cars, and sold stamps and golf balls."

Buffett's father was elected to represent Nebraska in the United States Congress in 1942. The Buffett family moved to the Washington, D.C. area so that his father could begin his new position. Buffett finished elementary school there and then attended Alice Deal Junior High School, followed by Woodrow Wilson High School in the nation's capitol.

Buffett's business activities continued after the move to Washington. During his high school years, he made an extraordinary amount of money for someone his age. He delivered newspapers, detailed cars, and sold stamps and golf balls, among other things. In 1944, at the age of 13, he filed his first income tax return. He took a $35 deduction, claiming the costs of his bicycle and his watch, which were used on his paper delivery route, as business expenses.

The next year, Warren found another business opportunity. Along with a friend, he purchased a second-hand pinball machine costing $25. This machine was placed in a D.C. barber shop for the use of customers. In a matter of months, Buffett and his friend had branched out, owning three pinball machines in three different shops.

Buffett didn't just earn money. He also scrupulously saved what he earned, only spending to reinvest in his own small business ventures.

> "He also scrupulously saved what he earned, only spending to reinvest in his own small business ventures."

Warren Buffett was not terribly keen on the idea of going to university, but his father wanted him to continue his education. He was already a businessman, and was making good money. He had saved over $5,000 from his high school work, mostly delivering newspapers. In 1947, that was a lot of money even for an adult, the equivalent of over $40,000 today, as a rough estimate in either US or Australian dollars. He was interested in going into business full-time.

Warren's father, however, wanted the young man to continue his education. Reluctantly, but dutifully, the 16-year-old Buffett began attending the University of Pennsylvania's Wharton Business School.

Buffett studied there for two years. After four terms in the US congress, Howard Buffett, Warren's father, lost the next election and returned to Omaha. Warren followed, transferring to the University of Nebraska-Lincoln. The next year, having studied hard, Buffett graduated a year early, with a B.S. in Economics.

Encouraged once again by his father, and against his own inclinations, Buffett applied to Harvard Business School, but was rejected because he was too young. Buffett soon found reason to be glad of this, because he then enrolled at Columbia Business School. Buffett followed his own interests here, despite his lack of enthusiasm for more schooling. He had learned that Benjamin Graham and David Dodd both taught classes at Columbia. These two, particularly Graham, were men whom Buffett admired. Graham had written, among others, a book entitled *The Intelligent Investor*. Buffett had read this book, and calls it "the greatest book on investing ever written".

Graham would become Buffett's mentor, and the investing principles described by Graham would influence Buffett's whole career. The basic idea was to value a company, not only by its value on the stock exchange, but by using stock prices to compare to the intrinsic value. This "intrinsic value" was a way of calculating the real worth of a company, completely outside of its share prices. By comparing stock prices to intrinsic value, an investor could then look for undervalued stocks to purchase whose prices would eventually rise due to the intrinsic value. This calculation, combined with assessing and judging a wide margin of safety, could point investors to good calculated risks, rather than simply gambling on the exchange and hoping for the best.

Buffett's reluctance to continuing with his education was not due to lack of academic ability, nor did it lead to lackadaisical study methods on the part of the young student. He did not do anything halfway. He slammed through his courses, graduating in 1951 with an M.S. in Economics, the only Columbia student ever to receive the highest possible marks in one of Graham's classes. He also attended the New York Institute of Finance. Buffett had continued to scrimp and save, and by the time he graduated from college, he had banked $9,800, which was worth roughly ten times that amount in today's dollars.

A curious incident that took place while Buffett was at Columbia illustrates his aggressive and determined approach. He learned that Graham was on the board of a company called GEICO insurance. He hopped on a train to Washington, D.C., arriving on a Saturday. He knocked on the door of GEICO's headquarters until he was eventually let in by a janitor. He wandered in, and found that the Vice President of GEICO, Lorimer Davidson, was in the office that day. Buffett immediately began asking about the insurance business, and the two ended up talking for hours. Davidson has since said that he knew within 15 minutes of starting this conversation that he was talking to an extraordinary man. This was the beginning of a lasting friendship between the two.

After graduating from Columbia, Buffett's wish was to go to work at the New York Stock Exchange. Both Buffett's father and Benjamin Graham discouraged this notion. Warren then offered to come to work for Graham at the Graham-Newman Corporation, but was initially turned down.

So, Buffett returned to his hometown of Omaha, Nebraska, in 1951. He first worked as an investment salesman at Buffett-Falk & Co., his father's brokerage firm. He then received a call from Benjamin Graham, offering him a position as a securities analyst at the Graham-Newman Corporation, where Buffett had previously offered to work for free, just to get his foot in the door. He promptly accepted the job and moved to New York in 1954.

He took his wife with him, having married Susan Thompson two years earlier in Nebraska, and their first child, Susan Alice. The move was worthwhile, since Warren would be mentored by his idol, and also for the high starting salary. While at Graham-Newman, Buffett received a thorough schooling in the methods of his mentor, both absorbing and questioning the investment principles. Although his strategy is mostly derived from Graham's, young Buffett did wonder whether insisting on huge margins of safety was causing the firm to miss some really big-paying opportunities.

In 1956, when Buffett had been at the company for two years, Graham retired, closing the doors of the partnership. In the meantime, Warren and Susan had their second child. His growing family certainly did not slow Buffett down, as he had already amassed a small fortune, and was comfortably well-off by this time.

Buffett returned to Omaha once again. Here he began his own investment partnership, Buffett Partnership Ltd. From then on, Buffett worked for himself, opening seven investment partnerships over the next several years. These were soon consolidated into one partnership.

In 1957, Buffett decided to purchase a home in Omaha. He was doing well, to say the least, and chose a place for himself and his growing family. Warren and Susan were expecting their third child by this time, and Buffett chose a stucco house in Omaha with five bedrooms. He paid $31,500 for this house. The family took up residence there. This has been Warren Buffett's home ever since.

Buffett continued to expand, becoming a very wealthy man. In 1962, Buffett began purchasing shares in what would become the centre point of his empire, Berkshire Hathaway. This company was a textile manufacturer whose shares Buffett had identified as undervalued. By 1963, Buffett had a controlling interest in the company. He installed a new manager to run the textile manufactory and interested himself in the company's financial side. He began expanding the financial side of the business, using the company as his main investment vehicle. Berkshire was mainly used for purchasing insurance companies. The financial side continued to grow, and Berkshire Hathaway operated with parallel roles of textiles and investments. Eventually, the manufacturing operations ceased in the 1980's, but Berkshire Hathaway remains Buffett's investment firm.

He continued to do business this way over the following decades. In 1977, Buffett was devastated when his wife, Susan, left him. Although they never divorced, and continued with an amicable relationship, Susan moved out, leaving for San Francisco. They continued to be close, speaking on the telephone and sharing their annual family vacation together, and spending time together with their three children, but Susie simply wanted to be on her own. As odd as it sounds, she introduced Buffett to other women in Omaha, trying to find him a companion. She set him up with a waitress named Astrid Merks, with whom Buffett developed a close relationship. With the blessings of Buffett's wife, Merks later moved into Warren's Omaha home, and the couple have been together ever since.

Buffett has not stopped buying and selling full-time since the day he started his own partnership. He has invested in or purchased countless companies through Berkshire Hathaway. Some of his best-known investments and acquisitions include *The Washington Post*, ABC network, GEICO, where his former mentor Graham had worked, and *Coca-Cola*. Throughout most of this time, he lived on his relatively low salary, keeping his assets in company stock. His net worth grew into the tens of thousands, then into the millions, then into the billions, and finally reached the stratospheric levels that made him the world's richest man in 2009.

> "...finally reached the stratospheric levels that made him the world's richest man in 2009."

Through it all, the "Oracle of Omaha" continued to live a fairly simple, frugal life. He simply has little taste for extravagance. His real passion is the game of making money, not spending it. He lives very frugally and has simple tastes. Buffett used commercial air travel until 1986, when his high profile finally made public travel so inconvenient that he finally bought a private plane. The aircraft that he purchased cost $850,000. In true Warren Buffett style, the airplane was a used one, and a bargain at the price. He enjoys following and supporting local college sports. He also spends about 12 hours per week on playing bridge, partnering up with friends like Bill Gates, another of the world's wealthiest people.

Wealth Accumulation

> "... at the age of 16, he was worth $5000."

Warren Edward Buffett began growing his wealth almost as soon as he was old enough to walk to school by himself. By the time the young Buffett had graduated from high school at the age of 16, he was worth $5000. By the time he graduated from university, he had $9800 in savings.

When he went to work for Graham, he started at a then-high salary of over $12,000, or close to $100,000 US translated into today's money. During the formative years at the New York investment firm, Buffett's investment strategy was solidified. He took Graham's investment philosophy of comparing intrinsic to actual trading values, and expanded on it. Warren studied more than the figures. He began to look for companies that he believed in, based on how they operated. He started paying attention to how the companies that he was considering were run, paying attention to management and leadership styles to see if he believed the corporations were on the right track.

By the time Buffett left Graham-Newman, he had built his own wealth to the sum of $140,000 US. This was all before he ever owned his own firm.

Once he went into business for himself, his already more-than-respectable wealth really took off. His partnerships profited 251% over the first five years, outperforming the stock market by over three times.

In 1962, six years after returning to Omaha from New York, Buffett had made his first personal million. His partnerships had grown in value to over $7 million dollars, with Buffett holding just over one million in personal holdings. Buffett merged all of the partnerships into one at this time.

Buffett always tended to do what everyone else was not doing. In 1964, a scandal caused shares of a certain financial company to drop to very low levels, with people liquidating assets in fear of the fraud investigation that was brewing. When shares had dropped to a low $35, Buffett started to purchase the shares in large numbers, deciding that the company was due to rebound. The company was American Express. The stock prices more than doubled in a single year.

In 1969, Buffett liquidated this partnership, transferring the assets to shareholders. He took the seat of chairman of Berkshire Hathaway in 1970, and this is when he began writing his annual letter to shareholders, which have become a famous Buffett tradition. Even though he was making enormous sums by investment, considering that Berkshire stock was now worth $290 per share, and despite his millionaire status, he lived primarily within the means of his annual salary, which paid him $50,000 per year. In fact, although Buffett was by then worth about $140 million, he was a poor little rich man. It is reported that he commented to a broker at the time, "Everything I got is tied up in Berkshire. I'd like a few nickels outside."

Buffett began increasing his purely personal investments, since his assets were really the shares of Berkshire. He speculated far less conservatively with his personal cash than he did with his business, but he was no less prescient. He quickly made three million dollars in outside personal income purely by playing the market.

In 1974, Berkshire's value fell, and Buffett's personal fortune was more than cut in half. Stock prices were falling, and Buffett's own holdings were not immune. Instead of panicking, Buffett, as usual, saw an opportunity the previous year to buy shares cheaply and Berkshire continued to increase its holdings. Not surprisingly, stock values eventually rebounded. Buffett had learned patience after his first market foray, all the way back at the age of 11.

By 1979, Berkshire shares continued to grow, and Buffett held many other profitable investments. That year, he made the Forbes 400, placing him among the wealthiest men in the nation. At that time, he was worth $620 million. This is when he began buying shares in ABC.

In 1983, Buffett began buying shares of Nebraska Furniture Mart. Although this name does not carry the same recognisable weight with most people that *The Washington Post*, GEICO, or *Coca-Cola* does, it nonetheless would turn out to be one of Berkshire Hathaway's most profitable investments. This was a purely local investment. Rose Blumpkin was a Russian immigrant. "Mrs. B", as she was known locally in Nebraska, had started a retail furniture store, and grown it into a multi-million dollar business. This was possibly one of the simplest business deals ever made. When approached to see if she was willing to sell, she simply replied that, yes, she would sell the business for $60 million. The deal concluded with a handshake and a one-page contract, after which Mrs. B is reported to have folded the check without looking at the number, and put it in her pocket. She had walked away rich, and the business would make Buffett even richer.

In 1988, Buffett started to purchase stock in *Coca-Cola*, which would be one of his largest earners.

Buffett's career has not been entirely smooth sailing. He has faced downturns in the market, as well as court hearings and scandals that have rocked Berkshire Hathaway and Buffett himself. He was eventually cleared of wrongdoing on all, and his investments have always come back. He rode out all of these storms, legal and financial, in his characteristic calm, Midwestern style.

In the recent recession, Buffett took his hits along with everyone else. During the third quarter of 2008, Berkshire Hathaway earnings dropped by 77%. Buffett responded by buying shares of GE Corporation and Goldman-Sachs, companies that no one else would touch, given their central place in the American economic crisis and subsequent bailout. Of course, that's how Buffett has always done things. If he'd done things the way everyone else did them, he wouldn't be Warren Buffett.

> "He had finally surpassed his friend Bill Gates, with a net worth of around $60 billion."

Buffett's investment style is deceptively simple, and usually very focused. It is standard investment advice to diversify one's holdings to protect against losses. Buffet takes the opposite approach, purchasing relatively few holdings for such a large investor. Instead of spreading his money out, he very selectively looks at corporations, and invests big when he decides to make a move. He says that, "Diversification is a protection against ignorance. It makes little sense for those who know what they're doing."

The contrary investor has also famously stayed away from the tech sector, even when the young computer industry was churning out billionaires at an astonishing rate. Although he regularly takes calculated risks, and moved away from the extreme caution of Graham's approach, he still concerns himself with margins of safety. And he decided that tech simply did not have this safe edge. It is a quirky twist of fate that, while avoiding tech stocks in investing, he developed a close personal friendship with Mr. Tech himself, Bill Gates. In fact, Buffett made Gates director of the Property & Casualty Insurance sector at Berkshire Hathaway Inc. And when it comes to giving money away, Buffett is going straight to the tech mind. He has pledged most of his mind-boggling fortune to the Bill and Melinda Gates Foundation.

Buffett's net worth reached billionaire status long before the financial crisis, back in 1990. Berkshire had begun selling class A shares. In 2008, Forbes listed Warren Buffett as the world's wealthiest man. He had finally surpassed his friend Bill Gates, with a net worth of around $60 billion.

Achievements and Foundations

Warren Buffett has always been a self-starter. He learned how to make good money on a small scale as a child and very young man, selling bottles of cola, delivering newspapers, selling gum, and purchasing that pinball machine for $25. The three-pinball machine business was sold by the young Buffett and his friend to a war veteran for $1200.

He always had a gift for simple figures, being the prodigy who could add long columns of numbers in his head. He still occasionally amuses and astonishes friends with this little trick. The gifted boy grew into one of the richest men in the world.

Buffett is, of course, highly sought after for advice. He has always famously refused to give stock tips. He insists that people need to invest according to their own principles. He is quite generous, however, with advice on those principles. His life and his speech reflect his way of bucking trends. He says to "be fearful when others are greedy and greedy when others are fearful". Early on, the news that Buffett had purchased shares in a certain company would cause that company's stock to rise by up to 10%.

There have been an astonishing number of books written about Buffett. His advice is highly sought-after. He is a very personable man, who combines seriousness and humour in his speech and writing. His letters to stockholders are gems that are widely read and quoted, by investors and others.

His public recognition had grown to a large extent by the 1980s. He has been widely sought and studied. Both John McCain and

Barack Obama mentioned their interest in him as a possible Secretary of the Treasury. Buffett was a finance advisor to Arnold Schwarzenegger during his 2003 campaign for Governor of California.

Buffett was named the top money manager of the twentieth century in 1999. This was in a Carson Group survey. In 2007, *Time* magazine named Buffett in their list of the 100 Most Influential People in the world.

> "Buffett was named the top money manager of the twentieth century."

Buffett turned his attention to philanthropy in the 1980s. He has long intended to simply give away the vast majority of his fortune. His wife, Suzie, was set to inherit a large part of that fortune had Buffett predeceased her. Her death in 2004 changed that. Buffett's three children will inherit only a small part of his money. He told a NY Times interviewer, "I don't believe in dynastic wealth". He is true to his word. He once said that "I want to give my kids just enough so that they would feel that they could do anything, but not so much that they would feel like doing nothing."

> "I want to give my kids just enough so that they would feel that they could do anything, but not so much that they would feel like doing nothing"

Early on, he started a philanthropic foundation, the Buffett Foundation. The foundation was actually established in 1964, but efforts were increased in the 1980s. In 1987, the Foundation was appointed its first director. Allen Greenberg was married to Buffett's daughter, Susie, at the time. They divorced in 1995, but Greenberg still retains the executive director's position. He originally intended that most of his fortune would go to the charity after his death. His wife, who died in 2004, left about $2.5 billion to the organisation. Among the foundation's benefactors are Planned Parenthood, the World Food Programme, and scholarships in Buffett's home state of Nebraska.

Buffett eventually changed his charitable tactics. He announced in 2006 that he intended to give most of his money away while he is still alive. He pledged 83% of his fortune to the Bill and Melinda Gates foundation. The donation was worth nearly $30 billion. This was the largest charitable donation ever made. The complicated transfer of such huge sums is annualised, with 5% of the donation going to the fund, starting in 2006. Buffet had decided to join the venture capitalism movement. He says that he had grown to admire what the Gates Foundation was doing, and believes in its effectiveness since the Foundation was already launched on a large scale.

> "The donation was worth nearly $30 billion."

Buffett is charitable in smaller, quirkier ways, too. He auctioned off his five-year-old Lincoln Town Car on eBay, giving the proceeds to the Girls, Inc. organisation. He has also auctioned off a luncheon and a dinner with himself, with winning bidders paying between $1.6 and $2.1 million dollars to share a meal with Buffett, and the proceeds going to charity.

The most recent (as of 2010) Forbes' ranking shows the Sage of Omaha's ranking at number three in the world. His most recent net worth, according to Forbes, is $47 billion. The shares of Berkshire Hathaway are back up after the downturn, although the recovery is slow. Buffett has slipped from the number one spot that he held in 2008. He has been once again surpassed by his friend, Bill Gates, as well as another investor from Mexico who recently rose to the No#1 spot. Some of the slip, at least, can be attributed to the fact that part of Buffett's fortune has gone to Gates' charity, although Gates himself is a major donator to charity as well. But the two have remained close on the Forbes' list for many years, with people following them to see which of the two will come out on top each year.

Buffett has achieved a great deal, and continues to do business, although he is now approaching his 80th birthday. When he was of an age where his peers concentrated on little but their first years of school, and playtime, Buffett was out working to make money. Now that he's reached an age where most people have long since retired, he continues to do so.

Warren Buffett's Tips for Success

By now, the modus operandi of the self-made billionaire is becoming apparent, and Warren Buffett epitomises the type. His life story is a study in goals, single-minded focus and hard work. Buffett got started even younger than most. He, along with Richard Branson, are notable for beginning their first business ventures at the tender age of 6.

> "The 'billionaire next door' lives a quiet and regular life, including what remains a 60-hour work week."

Buffett has risen steadily through life, increasing his net worth almost every year since he began. What started with a few items resold from his grandfather's grocery store in Omaha has turned into $49 billion dollars in investment holdings. 'The billionaire next door' lives a quiet and regular life, including what remains a 60-hour work week, punctuated by bridge games.

He is also one of the most sought-after financial gurus in the world. Everyone, big and small, prince and pauper, president and average citizen, would like a piece of Buffett's wisdom. His life and his approach, despite the complexities of economics and the stock market, demonstrate a beautiful simplicity of approach.

- This simplicity is the first lesson that we can take from the Buffett approach. He grasps a few simple facts and figures, and makes his investment decisions on the same principles over and over. He has not changed his approach in any essential way since about 1950, upon first reading Graham's book.

He is a principled investor who looks for fundamental values. These values are both financial and less tangible. He looks for integrity in business leadership and advises people to "invest according to your convictions".

- He approaches each investment with the idea of a long-term holding. One gem of Buffett advice is to "only buy something that you'd be perfectly happy to hold if the market shut down for 10 years". Far from the shotgun diversification approach taken by most investors, Buffett's method is one of selection, rather than pure acquisition. In the same vein, he says, "Our favourite holding period is forever." And again, "Someone's sitting in the shade today because someone planted a tree a long time ago."

- The extreme simplicity of Buffett's financial advice points up the fact that most people probably ignore the true fundamentals. Those who build enormous wealth are able to focus on letting those fundamentals drive everything they do, no matter how complex the actions become. A few pearls on investing from Buffett illustrate this point: "Patience pays—buy 'em and hold' em." "Invest in businesses you understand." "Buy at a reasonable price." "Look for honest, able management." These are the basic tenets of Buffett's personal strategy. They contain simple, common-sense thinking with integrity.

Buffett gave a hugely popular interview in recent years to CNBC. This interview was full of his characteristic humour and hard-headed common sense. When asked, "What is the Warren Buffett secret to success?" his reply was;

- "If people get to my age and they have the people love them that they want to have love them, they're successful.

It doesn't make any difference if they've got a thousand dollars in the bank or a billion dollars in the bank.... Success is really doing what you love and doing it well. It's as simple as that. I've never met anyone doing that who doesn't feel like a success. And I've met plenty of people who have not achieved that and whose lives are miserable."

To repeat: "Success is really doing what you love and doing it well. It's as simple as that." In other words, follow your passion and work hard at it to make it good. This basic concept is a principle that underlies the strategy of every success story that we've seen. There might be luck, accidents, or specific ideas that play a big part in success, but they all derive from that simple idea.

> "Success is really doing what you love and doing it well. It's as simple as that."

- Buffett doesn't seem to have ever spent a waking moment (or perhaps a sleeping one) without having business on his mind. However, his predilection for movies, sports games, and bridge demonstrate that he does take time off to relax. Yet, one gets the impression that calculations are simply a part of his brain's wiring, and might be running in the background even when he is thinking about something else. He acts with a calm certainty that makes him the unstoppable force of investments. He has said, "I always knew I was going to be rich. I don't think I ever doubted it for a minute."

Buffett just might be the steadiest performer of any kind in human history. His life is a single, continuous course of simple living, simple pleasures and making money. There is a truly Zen feel to his progress through life. He seems to have kept a quiet, steady, progressively building course the whole time.

- Warren Buffett also points out that the company that a person keeps can affect their success. If you want to be successful, rich or virtuous, seek out like-minded people—even people who have made more progress than you have. Warren Buffett most famously did that when he went to GEICO headquarters, knocking on the doors on a Saturday until he was allowed in. Warren says, "It's better to hang out with people better than you. Pick out associates whose behaviour is better than yours and you'll drift in that direction."

  This idea is not the most frequently mentioned, but it could be very important. People who succeed, at some point, have met at least one person who becomes a friend or associate who opens doors for them.

- Buffett also has insights into behaviour. He advises that acting with an eye to your company's reputation is important: "It takes 20 years to build a reputation and five minutes to ruin it. If you think about that, you'll do things differently." We can probably all think of people who rose to fame and fortune, only to be brought down by a scandal arising from pointless and thoughtless actions.

- There is another simple insight that Buffett offers, that certainly can be applied to investing. However, it also has much broader applications. Warren says that "Price is what you pay. Value is what you get." His is a mind that can estimate costs, not in terms of what a budget might allow in the moment, but in terms of the benefits that any purchase will bring in the future.

- Let's revisit the notion of simplicity. It really is the cornerstone of Buffett's approach, in life as in business. In this context, two more statements apply. "The business schools reward difficult complex behaviour more than simple behaviour, but simple behaviour is more effective." When Buffett was a reluctant college student, he complained that he knew more than his teachers. This might have sounded boastful, but his statement was certainly borne out by history. He also says, "There seems to be some perverse human characteristic that likes to make easy things difficult." His own pattern of behaviour certainly follows simple rules. He doesn't overcomplicate things.

Summary

The life of Warren Edward Buffett provides a beautifully clear example for anyone looking for strategies to success and fortune. For almost 75 years, Buffett has pursued a rather subdued, quiet course of moneymaking that has resulted in one of the largest single fortunes ever earned in human history. He simply loves to do business and has done little else with his time. He strikes one as a vessel of quiet satisfaction and steady purpose.

Yet he remains a kind, everyday sort of person in many ways. He is humorous and avuncular, always polite. He still lives in a rather modest house in the peaceful Midwestern town where he was born and raised.

From Warren Buffett's example, the principle of simplicity stands out. Start simple and stay simple. Simple in principles, simple in purpose and simple in tactics. Buffett's strategy has not really changed in the last 50 years. He has made his methods known to everyone who has asked, but no one has succeeded in the way that he has. Warren has always been able to add simple sums better and faster than anyone else. That special talent applies to more than simply numbers on a page.

It also applies to everything else that he does. He is a man with perfect clarity of purpose. He can look through the impossible welter of facts, figures and analysis, and see the true sum of a person, or of a business. He uses these simple ideas day in and day out, coupled with hard work, to keep his wealth and happiness growing.

"Leadership in a nutshell
- Clarity, Congruency,
Consistency, and Conveying
a sense of Certainty and
Inspiring Commitment."

Spike Humer

Darren sharing the stage with
Jim Rohn America's Leading
Business Philosopher

Bestselling Author Deepak Chopra
talking on Health & Spiritualism

eBay millionaire
Amanda Clarkson
and Spike Humer

Darren with Salle & James Redfield Author of The Celestine Prophecy

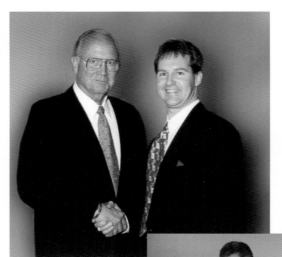

Darren with United
States Army General
Norman Schwarzkopf,
commander of the
Coalition Forces
in the Persian Gulf
War discussing his
leadership strategy's

Jay Abraham and
Spike Humer enjoying
Japan's fine food

Millionaires Spike Humer, Matt Clarkson and Darren Stephens smile for the media

America's No#1 Marketing experts, Jay Abraham and Spike Humer on tour in Asia

BestSelling Author Wayne Dwyer

Darren just loves his Merc

Darren and his wife, Jackie, arriving at their tropical island beach house

Darren holding the
Famous FA World
Soccer Cup at
Wembley Stadium
United Kingdom

Spike in action with
sold out crowds

Spike Humer receives the publishing
industry's Bestseller Award

Darren, Jackie & John Gray in front the Trevi fountain Rome

Darren Stephens and eBay's
Managing Director Deborah Sharkey

eBay's Australian Managing Director, Deborah
Sharkey, sharing her multimillion dollar online
success secrets

World-leading NLP and Hypnosis experts, Darren Stephens and Dr. Richard Bandler

Queen of Rock - Suzi Quatro - and Darren Stephens in Essex, London

Darren working hard at his Hamilton Island beach house!!

Darren Stephens and eBay millionaire, Matt Clarkson, at Google Inc.
Head Office, USA

Darren Stephens at eBay's corporate head office, CA, USA

Jordan Belfort, author of "The Wolf of Wall Street", and Darren Stephens

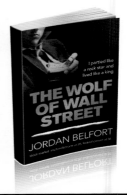

Best Selling Authors sharing ideas. Robert Allen – Author of "One Minute Millionaire" - with Darren Stephens

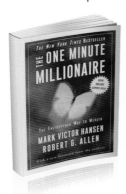

Darren and Jackie Stephens, Matt and Amanda Clarkson and Spike Humer celebrating Dr. Richard Bandler's Birthday – Orlando, Florida, USA

Former US President Bill Clinton and Darren Stephens talking leadership

Darren donating a $15,000 cheque raised for the Starlight Foundation from work done with his eBay business partners Matt and Amanda Clarkson

Darren and Spike having dinner with former UK Prime Minster Tony Blair

Darren, Andrew & Daryl Grant with there First Bestselling Author Group

Darren & Veronica Tan
signing books in Korea

The worlds Largest Event
Promoter & Asian Business
Leader, Multi Millionaire
Richard Tan

Darren & Jo Munro
sharing a Drink at
the famous Tom
Cruise Top Gun bar
in USA

Millionaire executive coach John Gearon Receives the International Coaching Award

Jackie & Darren Stephens sharing some laughs with Joseph McClendon III in Singapore

Authors & Speakers Ron Kaufman Darren Stephens & Blair Singer

Author & Billionaire Keith & Sandi Cunningham

Tony Blair

*"The art of leadership is saying no,
not saying yes. It is very easy to say yes."*

MILLIONAIRES & BILLIONAIRES

SECRETS REVEALED!

Brief Overview

Tony Blair

Born:	6th May, 1953, in Edinburgh, Scotland
Business:	Consultant , Former British Prime Minister
Industry:	Government, Politics
Income:	Estimated, variously, at anywhere from £20 million to £60 million
Lives:	London, UK
Family:	Wife, Cherie, and 4 children, Evan, Nicky, Katherine and Leo
Charities:	Tony Blair Faith Foundation, Tony Blair Sports Foundation and the Tony Blair Africa Governance Initiative
Status:	Millionaire

Tony Blair

Profile

Tony Blair is an example of how to reach great heights in politics. He served as British Prime Minister for 10 years, the only Labour Prime Minister to serve consecutive terms. He took his party to this position by making changes from the inside.

Under his leadership, the Labour Party adopted its "New Labour" bent, appealing more to the centre and thereby amassing enough support to bring himself and his party to victory. He began his rapid rise among political ranks shortly after completing his education. He did not stop until he reached the highest office he could hold.

He has great popular appeal and mixed his convictions with his public life. Since he served as Prime Minister, he has entered the world of finance. Blair has now amassed a fortune. He joined a financial company as advisor at a large salary. Much of his income arises from the large fees he can now collect for public speaking engagements. In addition, he has income from property investments.

Tony Blair, the young man from Edinburgh, made his way all the way to 10 Downing Street. He remains an activist to this day, and a man very much in the public eye.

Background

Anthony Charles Lynton Blair was born on 6th May, 1953, in Edinburgh, Scotland. He was the second of three children born to Leo and Hazel Blair. When Tony was born, his father was studying for his law degree at the University of Edinburgh, and working as a tax inspector. When Tony Blair was still less than two years old, his father graduated and moved the family to Adelaide, Australia, having accepted a teaching position as law lecturer at the University of Adelaide.

The family was there for a little over three years, before returning to Britain and settling in Durham, England, again because his father had accepted a new teaching position. Young Tony attended school there, starting at The Chorister School in 1961. Five years later, Tony began his term at Fettes College, boarding at the Edinburgh school. At that time, young Blair rather fancied himself as a rock star of some kind, being interested in music, and was a fan of Mick Jagger.

Blair was a bit of a rebel during that phase. His teachers reportedly thought him something of a pain and he was even arrested during his time there. He was attempting to climb back into his room late at night and raised alarms because he was mistaken for a burglar.

When Blair finished at Fettes, he then moved to London. He was still, at this time, interested in a career in rock music. He first tried to become a rock music promoter, but eventually settled down enough to return to school, attending St. John's College, Oxford. Even there, he played for a while in a rock band.

While at Oxford, Tony Blair met the man who would have a major influence on his ideas. Although raised with a common religious or church view, Blair didn't seem to take it more seriously than any other boy. After meeting Peter Thompson, an Anglican priest and fellow Oxford student, this began to change. The friendship between the two was highly influential on Blair, who developed deep religious beliefs, as well as far-left political views. Blair's Oxford years were marred by the death of his mother from cancer.

In 1976, Blair graduated from Oxford with a Second Class Honours BA in Jurisprudence. Blair then began practicing law as a pupil barrister. He also joined the Labour Party at this time. While practicing as a barrister, he met Cherie Booth at chambers. The two were married in 1980. The couple eventually had four children.

It was during the 80s that Blair began his true political career. His first attempts at seeking positions were unsuccessful, but he began to make a name for himself in the party. At this time, Blair was firmly in the Socialist camp, and only later moved to a more centrist stance. In 1983, a constituency had been created at Sedgefield, near Durham, where he had spent much of his childhood. Blair sought and won the selection, and took his seat in the House of Commons. The following year, he received a front-bench appointment, and had started his rapid ascent through the political system.

By the latter half of the 1980s, Blair had placed himself within the reformist camp of his party. The 1987 election was followed by Blair's appointment to the Shadow Cabinet. He became a persistent and highly visible advocate for the Labour Party's movement from the far left to closer to the centre position and to relax its position on public ownership of production and total state control.

John Smith became leader of the party in 1992 and appointed Blair to the position of shadow Home Secretary. Two years later, following Smith's sudden death, Blair was elected party leader. Blair went to work reforming his party, leading it to a somewhat more moderate position on many issues, and changing one clause of its constitution. The New Labour party, as Blair called it, had greater popular appeal and won most municipal elections in

1995. In 1997, Labour again roundly defeated the conservatives in the general election, making Tony Blair Prime Minister of the United Kingdom.

At 43 years old, Tony Blair was the UK's youngest prime minister in 185 years. He would also be re-elected three times after that, making him the Labour party's only candidate to ever be elected in three consecutive wins. He was also the longest-serving PM from Labour.

During his term, he played a large role in the Northern Ireland Peace Process and was a staunch supporter of US president George Bush's War on Terror after the September 11 terrorist attacks on the World Trade Center.

"At 43 years old, Tony Blair was the UK's youngest prime minister in 185 years."

Blair was wildly popular for most of his stint as prime minister. His popularity began to decline in Britain after his last election, most notably due to his unpopular foreign policy stance in the Iraq war. After ten years as Prime Minister, Blair tendered his resignation.

When Blair left office in 2007, he became the Middle East envoy for the United Nations, European Union, the United States and Russia. In 2008, Blair also became a senior advisor to JPMorgan Chase and a climate change advisor to Zurich Financial Services.

He also took his place on the lecture circuit, commanding large fees for public speaking, and accepted a position to teach at Yale University in the States.

Starting in 2007, Blair set up charity foundations to promote several of his particular areas of passion. The Tony Blair Sports Foundation promotes health in children, the Tony Blair Faith Foundation aims to raise cooperation among different faiths, and he set up a charity called the Tony Blair Africa Governance Initiative.

Blair's rise to the seats of power was rapid and strong. He held the office of prime minister for longer than any other Labour leader, after working tirelessly to reform his party. He brought Labour into a new age, and gave it a position of broad popular appeal. His was a strong presence on the world stage during his terms and he is still highly active in foreign relations. He is best known for his party reform efforts, his foreign policy stance and his strong religious faith. He has a gift for appearing to good advantage in public and is regarded as a charismatic speaker with plenty of presence.

Wealth Accumulation

Since leaving office, work has been lucrative for Blair. He gets paid enormous sums for public speaking, earning six figures for each lecture. When he joined JPMorgan Chase, it has been reported that he began earning a salary of over £500,000 per year. He also has property investments that bring him an income.

Tony Blair's wealth is rather a mystery and the subject of much speculation. For most of his life, he has obviously concentrated on gaining political clout, and not on producing an income. The main lessons to be learned about success from Blair are about his rise to power.

His finances and their sources are hidden in obscurity. He has many income streams. His *Tony Blair Associates* is a consultancy firm. When he signed the deal to produce his memoirs, *A Journey*, the book deal brought him many millions of pounds. The advance on the book was £4.6 million.

He also has incomes through charitable organisations, in addition to religious ones. So convoluted are the former PM's financial arrangements that *The Guardian*, at the end of 2009, offered a prize to anyone who could help elucidate the various sources of Blair's wealth. *The Guardian* says that, "Blair has a complex web of structures involving 12 different legal entities handling the unprecedented millions he is receiving since he stepped down from office in 2007."

"So mystifying are the former prime minister's financial structures – which involve highly specialised limited partnerships and parallel companies – that the Guardian today launches an open invitation to tax specialists and accountants to attempt to explain the motivation behind such structures."

Most of Blair's income has been funnelled through a company called Windrush Ventures. Another, similar company, Firerush Ventures, channels another. These companies are set up to handle all of the various sources of income, but the reason for it is a mystery, and Blair is not talking.

There are no accusations that Tony Blair is making any illegal financial deals. But he has kept the nature of his companies, such as limited partnerships, very secret, making it quite difficult to track the sources of his wealth.

In fact, his net worth is a mystery too, and it is only known that he is a multimillionaire. His Blair Incorporated is a parent company that is producing some unnamed revenues, employing 130 people.

Only two of Blair's companies filed accounts that are publicly available. In the financial year ending in 2009, the two companies combined earned £11.7 million, as reported by *Telegraph*. But even this income is corporate income and does not reflect Blair's personal earnings. His total income from combined sources now brings Blair over £7 million per year by some estimates.

His net worth has been estimated, variously, at anywhere from £20 million to £60 million. The Blairs certainly live like rich people. They have lavish homes with the finest furniture and they generally live in the lap of luxury.

He has said that his secrecy, at least in some cases, is due to the "commercially sensitive" nature of the business deals. He struck one deal with UI Energy Corporation, an oil firm in South Korea, that certainly was sensitive. It caused some talk when news of the deal leaked out after two years of silence. The oil company has interests in Iraq, which certainly raised eyebrows given Blair's stance on foreign policy.

Blair has regular sources of income stemming from his public service. He receives a publicly funded allowance for his office of £84,000 annually. He also has his pension, which provides £63,468 per year. However, given Blair's multimillion pound income, the majority of his financial arrangements lie in the mysterious companies.

However Blair accumulated his wealth, he now lives the life of the rich and famous. Much like Bill Clinton, Blair is cashing in on his political career, after leaving the premiership.

Blair's real story is one of how to capitalise and build success in public service. He made his mark early, after joining the Labour Party. He had a fortunate connection when he decided to make his bid for Parliament. His father-in-law was the original connection to Tom Pendry, Labour MP. It was Pendry who took Blair under his wing, giving him a tour of the House of Commons, and advising Blair to try for the seat of Beaconsfield. This was a Conservative seat, but Pendry knew a member of the party there. Although Blair was chosen as candidate, he lost the election, gaining only 10% of the vote.

This was not surprising, given the constituency, but the benefit was that his efforts drew the attention of Michael Foot, who was then leader of the Labour Party.

From then on, Blair did not stop. He held his seat until he stepped down from the prime minister's office, and accepted the Middle East Envoy position. Once he took the helm of the Labour Party, he made swift changes, which effectively revitalised the party, and swept it back into the majority.

Blair's effectiveness as a political leader is due, at least in part, to his talents in being a charismatic public figure. He is in command of the impression that he gives to the media. He had an image of being one of the people, speaking in his informal fashion.

Blair's ascent through politics was a mixture of the strong views that he formed while attending Oxford, and an apparent early wish to be famous. Remember, early on he wanted to be a rock star, and tried to gain fame as a promoter before pursuing his Oxford studies. His interest in politics doesn't seem to have started terribly early, but his interest in fame did. Of course, he did study law, indicating a possible interest in the workings of government.

In any case, he did learn a talent for presenting himself to the media. He was an excellent and persuasive public speaker then, and remains so today. Blair was able to take decisive action in moving the Labour Party toward its new status and was also able to then make swift and decisive action in moving to ever higher public offices.

Blair, like any high-profile political figure, has plenty of critics and detractors. His popularity did decline, and his critics still find issues to discuss. But, the fact remains that he did lead his party to the greatest number of successful victories in Labour history. He also was the longest-serving Labour prime minister.

No matter what mysteries surround Blair's wealth, his career since leaving the prime minister's office has been unquestioningly lucrative. No estimate of Tony Blair's wealth falls short of tens of millions of pounds. The convoluted array of ventures and businesses that prevent our examining his income do not hide the fact that Blair is a political and financial success.

Achievements and Foundations

The achievements of Tony Blair are numerous. As has already been mentioned, he led New Labour to the most successful run of victories in the party's history.

After his achievements in his political career, Blair went on to others in both the public and private sectors. He has achieved recognition for many of his accomplishments. Blair was the recipient of an honorary doctorate of law from Queen's University Belfast. This honour recognised his role in the peace negotiations in Northern Ireland, and was also for distinction in public service. He received this degree on 22nd May, 2008.

Blair's close ties to, and support of, the United States resulted in another honour on 13th January, 2009. US president George W. Bush presented the Presidential Medal of Freedom to Tony Blair. The American head of state cited Blair's role in Northern Ireland's peace process in addition to Blair's support of United States policy in response to the World Trade Center attacks, during the presentation "in recognition of exemplary achievement and to convey the utmost esteem of the American people."

Tel Aviv University presented Blair with the Dan David Prize in 2009. This honour was received in recognition of "exceptional leadership and steadfast determination in helping to engineer agreements and forge lasting solutions to areas in conflict."

More recognition is due to come to Tony Blair. On 30th June, 2010, an announcement was made by the president of the National Constitution Center, in Philadelphia, Pennsylvania, USA, that Blair would be the recipient of the 2010 Liberty Medal. The award is to be presented in September of 2010 by former President Bill Clinton, who is chair of the centre. This medal will be awarded "in recognition of his steadfast commitment to conflict resolution".

Blair's charitable activities have also been advanced since he left the prime minister's office. The Tony Blair Sports Foundation was set up to benefit children, with special focus on the North East. The Foundation is set up to encourage volunteering as sports coaches, to help make sport accessible to the children of the area. When the event was launched, Blair gave a speech, which said in part, "I have always been passionate about sport and its capacity to change people's lives. It is often the best public health policy, the best way to bring people together. When North East businesses sign up to my Sports Foundation's new scheme, their employees will have the opportunity to volunteer as sports coaches and officials, and in the process they will open up sport to even more young people in their local communities."

Blair also founded the Tony Blair Faith Foundation. The Foundation's mission statement says that "The Tony Blair Faith Foundation aims to promote respect and understanding about the world's major religions and show how faith is a powerful force for good in the modern world." Blair's religious convictions have played a major role in his development as a person and a leader, ever since his Oxford days. He eventually joined the Catholic Church, but his foreign policy experience convinced him that religious tolerance is important.

The Tony Blair Africa Governance Initiative is an organisation that was set up to try to improve conditions in the poor countries of Africa.

The aim is to work with state leaders to help them implement reform. The goals of the foundation are to help reduce poverty, implement government reforms and to "attract sustainable investment" to the region.

Blair's other most notable achievements are obviously the many acts and policy changes stemming from his office as Prime Minister. As has been mentioned, he was instrumental in bringing about the Good Friday Agreement, which brought an end to the Northern Ireland fighting. The agreement was signed in 1998.

His contribution to the Agreement remains one of Blair's most outstandingly popular works of diplomacy. He and others involved in the negotiation won wide acclaim for this work almost across the board. The praise for this peace process has come from high and low, from politicos, critics and the general populace.

He stands out clearly for his foreign policy, most notably during the invasions of Afghanistan and Iraq, but also for numerous other actions. Pledges that were implemented during his service as PM included the introduction of the minimum wage, the Freedom of Information Act, and the Human Rights Act.

Blair's terms also saw the devolution of the United Kingdom, with the establishment of separate regional bodies. These were the Northern Ireland Assembly, the Scottish Parliament, and the National Assembly for Wales.

Tony Blair launched himself into the political left with fervour. He has since brought the party from its far-left position and steered it in a new direction. The radical changes were made under his leadership. Although many supporters of Labour criticised these changes, feeling that the principles of the left had been abandoned, and claiming that he had moved the party to the right, he did find new supporters. He famously said about the changes, "I didn't come into politics to change the Labour Party. I came into politics to change the country." He then brought that party into the top office in Britain and kept it there for a decade. Afterward, he set up charitable foundations, serves as advisor to private companies and continues diplomatic work.

Tony Blair's Tips for Success

Tony Blair's example is, in some ways, one of trial-and-error. He did not, by any means, always seem destined for a highly successful political career. But he was always willing to stir things up and to try new things. He was not afraid to rock the boat and be a pain in the neck to authority, as evidenced from his days at boarding school. Even before his political ideals and aspirations came into being, he was playing with the idea of being a highly visible public speaker.

When he did start his political career, early failures did not faze him. He did not let some initially unsuccessful campaigns stop him for a minute. It was natural enough, in the highly polarised world of politics, that he would be both admired and vilified. It is a remarkable characteristic that he could be thick-skinned enough to handle criticism and support with aplomb. He drew both very early on, from inside and outside his own party.

Blair was invited to give a Class Day address at Yale University in 2008. During his speech, he attempted to summarise the wisdom that he had learned from his long experience. These lessons can apply to anyone, in any kind of career.

> "First...keep learning."

- "First...keep learning. Always be alive to the possibilities of the next experience, of thinking, doing and being." Tony Blair has always placed a great emphasis on the importance of learning. He famously told an audience that the top three issues of his administration would be "education, education, and education". Here, however, Blair is talking about more than formal schooling. He is discussing the way in which all of life is an educational experience, as long as people are open to it. One must continue to actively question and take lessons from every possible opportunity.

- "Be prepared to fail as well as succeed, and realise it is failure not success that defines character." We are used to hearing that failure is a good learning experience, that we can take lessons from failure. This is such common advice that it is ignored as a bromide. It is easy to hear this and nod in agreement. But it is perhaps far less common to take this advice to heart. In order to succeed, we must be prepared to fail sometimes. No one who has made it big has ever gone through life without failure. In fact, the bigger the success and the more visible the person, the more visible the failures. The only way to sustain motivation and self-esteem at such a level, when mistakes have big consequences and open a person up to public criticism, is to realise that those errors are not the ultimate verdict on a person's character or career. They are simply vivid examples of lessons to be learned.

> "Be prepared to fail as well as succeed, and realise it is failure not success that defines character."

- Tony Blair gets to a point that we have heard, in one type of phrasing or another, from every story that we have examined. "Above all... have a purpose in life. Life is not about living but about striving. When you get up, get motivated. Live with a perpetual sense of urgency." Here we get back to the crux of the matter. Call it purpose, passion, vision, or anything else, there is no success without it. It provides both a clear goal and the motivation to work for it. The other point is about "a perpetual sense of urgency". This idea translates into the motivation to put in the hard

> "No one who has made it big has ever gone through life without failure."

work to promote one's purpose, to strive to reach goals, every single day.

- Blair also points out that the difference between highly successful people and others is that the achievers take action, and other people talk about it. Or, in the context of leadership, "Be a doer not a commentator. Seek responsibility rather than shirk it. People often ask me about leadership. I say: leadership is about wanting the responsibility to be on your shoulders, not ignoring its weight but knowing someone has to carry it and reaching out for that person to be you. Leaders are heat-seekers, not heat-deflectors." The point here is that if people want to accomplish big things, they must bear large responsibility. Instead of fearing the consequences of this, welcome it. While such responsibilities will mean that mistakes will carry big consequences, it is also empowering. Accepting responsibility puts one in control. And being in the driver's seat, while it is more difficult and sometimes dangerous, is the only way to ensure that a person will reach the destination that they are aiming for.

> "... achievers take action, and other people talk about it."

Blair was invited to speak at the Olympic ceremony in Beijing. During this speech, the man known for his skills at oratory did not disappoint. He delivered his "What Makes a Champion" speech in such a way that he applied the ideas of athletics to everyday life. Widening the concept of achievement in sports to translate it into life lessons yielded some gems for anyone considering strategies for success.

- "...I chose to be a champion in a different field and it is also true that most people have innate talent at something. Champions are not just athletes. They are scientists, entrepreneurs, artists, philanthropists. They are people who the world sees in photos and on TV, people of fame and wealth. But they are just as often people no one outside a small circle has heard of...."

"So it is right that not everyone can be a champion. But many, perhaps even most of us, have the capacity to do something exceptionally well. Most of us have a gift."

> **"Most of us have a gift."**

"The issue is: how to develop that gift.... Because for sure, there is a part, perhaps even the major part of being a champion that is not to do with natural physique or natural intellect but is to do with character, attitude, the dimension of the mind that can be discovered and developed. You can improve."

"You can, in doing so, cross the line between the average and the good and in time even the line between the good and the outstanding."

This last points to, yet again, the essential need for constant effort and hard work. We don't need to be born with any mysterious, secret talents in order to succeed. We must just put what talents we do have to work and make every effort to develop, implement, and improve them. It is persistence in these efforts that will lead to success.

Summary

The example of Tony Blair is a case of character writ large. Love him or hate him, the fact is that, no matter what reaction he inspires, he does make an impression and have an effect. The lesson to be learned is that success is not the result of an effort to please everyone, but of forging ahead with outspoken force regardless of the reactions.

For those who make it big, and particularly those who do so in a highly visible way, a thick skin is essential. People can either do big things, or they can try to please everyone. They can't do both. One needs to be able to both accept and ignore criticism. Accept it as a possible source of learning, but ignore it when it threatens to stop your progress.

Blair has played out his life on a world stage for a long time now. He keeps going, in spite of obstacles, expertly walking the line between garnering the necessary support and pushing ahead despite detractors. He continues to put in that hard work, day in and day out. He is now reaping the reward of his efforts.

J.K. Rowling

*"It is our choices...that show what we truly are,
far more than our abilities."*

**MILLIONAIRES
& BILLIONAIRES**

SECRETS
REVEALED!

Brief Overview

J.K. Rowling

Born:	31st July, 1965, in Gloucestershire, UK
Business:	Author
Industry:	Publishing
Income:	Net worth $1 billion
Lives:	UK
Family:	Husband, Neil, and 3 children, Jessica, David and Mackenzie
Charities:	Children's High Level Group
Status:	Billionaire

J.K Rowling

Profile

The creator of *Harry Potter* has lived a life story that people are very fond of telling. We all love a rags-to-riches tale and Rowling's is particularly satisfying somehow. She went from toiling as a single mother to the status of multi-millionaire.

In the past decade, Rowling has risen from complete obscurity to world fame, fortune, and honour.

> "Harry Potter is a worldwide phenomenon."

Many people who make it big do so because they start young, and rise to fame and fortune through tireless work, but succeed early in life. But J.K. Rowling is a little bit different. Although she has loved to write stories since she was a child, she struggled to succeed until her 30s.

She is the first person to have made as much money, as she has, solely from writing books. But those books are clamoured for, demanded, thirsted for, and not merely by children. The stories of magic have indeed been magic for their author, as well as her young readers. *Harry Potter* is a worldwide phenomenon that will remain in the fond memories of children all over the world.

This series of books has made further fortunes in toys, movies, and even eyeglasses. Everyone can recognise the boy with the scar on his forehead and the wire-rimmed glasses and he exists only in fiction. His creator is now reaping the benefits.

Background

Joanne Rowling was born Gloucestershire, England, on 31st July, 1965. Her parents, Peter James Rowling and Anne Rowling, met when they were both on a train, journeying to join the Royal Navy. After their young marriage (both were 19), they moved to the Gloucestershire home, where Joanne was born. Joanne was their first child and their second, Dianne, was born just under two years later.

When Joanne was four years old, her family made a short-distance move to Winterbourne, also near Bristol. She began attending St. Michael's Primary School. Joanne and her sister were very active together, spending their time playing or, as Rowling says, "fighting like a pair of wildcats." Joanne once even threw a battery at her sister, Di, who did not duck as Joanne expected her to. The incident left Dianne with a scar on her forehead. No sketch of Harry Potter is complete without the telltale scar.

During breaks in the fighting, Joanne told her sister many stories, which turned into hours of play-acting. Joanne, or "Jo" as she was called, was able to bring tales vividly to life even at that tender age.

When Jo was nine years old, the Rowling family moved once more. Their new home was in Tutshill, near Wales.

Two years later, Rowling began attending Wyedean School and College, a secondary school. She began to enjoy the freedoms of growing up when she met a friend, Sean Harris, who had a car. Some of Rowling's favourite memories are of whizzing around the countryside in the Ford Angelina, the turquoise car that would later be driven by the fictional Ron Weasley in the stories.

Her friend Sean was also the first person that Joanne told about her ambitions of becoming a writer. Jo had been clear about her passion from a very young age, but she didn't speak freely about it. Jo's years at Wyedean were marked by a heavy emotional burden. Her mother, Anne, had been diagnosed with multiple sclerosis, and began a slow decline.

In 1983, Jo began attending the University of Exeter. She wanted to study English, but her parents encouraged her to study another language, considering it to be more practical. Rowling read French instead. Although she has some regrets about not sticking to her original desires, she was able to study for a year in Paris. She received her B.A. in French and Classics and moved to London. She held several jobs, the most notable of which was working with Amnesty International as a secretary, using her French skills.

Jo and her then-boyfriend were considering a move to Manchester in 1990, and had travelled up to go flat-hunting there. Jo returned to London by herself, on a four hour train ride. She has said that while on the train, the idea for the Harry Potter character simply came to her. She knew immediately that this was the next story she would write. Jo wanted to begin that very minute, but did not have a pen, and was too shy to borrow one from her fellow travellers. So, she mulled over her new idea for the entire train trip and began writing her story as soon as she arrived back in London. She has said, "I had been writing almost continuously since the age of six but I had never been so excited about an idea before."

Shortly after she began writing *Harry Potter*, Rowling's mother, Anne died of multiple sclerosis, ten years after she had first been diagnosed. This death deeply affected Rowling. It was a heavy loss and Rowling tells us that it was after this that Harry Potter's fully-dimensional feelings about his dead parents were fleshed out in her writing.

Rowling was so troubled by her mother's death that, in 1991, she needed a change of scene. She obtained a teaching job in Portugal, and left for sunnier climes, taking the Potter manuscript with her.

In Portugal, she met Jorge Arantes, a television journalist. They were married in 1992, and had a child, Jessica Isabel. The couple's relationship did not last, and they separated in 1993, only four months after Jessica was born.

One month later, Jo returned to Britain, now a single mother. She did not return to London. Instead, she moved to Edinburgh, where her sister Di now lived. Rowling intended to return to teaching. She knew that, as a working single mother, she might not have enough time to finish her book, so she worked furiously on the manuscript while she still did not have a teaching position. She was struggling on welfare at this time, but she still knew that this was her window of opportunity to complete the writing of the book. She would run to a cafe whenever her daughter was napping, working as hard as she could on the book, writing everything out in longhand. She then had to type up the entire manuscript. It was a brutal schedule, but Rowling managed to finish *Harry Potter and the Philosopher's Stone*. It was 1995, the year of Rowling's 30th birthday.

> "They began sending the book to publishers, but it was rejected by 12 separate houses."

> "Bloomsbury feared that the author's female name would prevent the book from appealing to boys."

The book was sent to Christopher Little Literary Agents, who liked the book and agreed to represent Jo. They began sending the book to publishers, but it was rejected by 12 separate houses. After a year of futile attempts, the book was accepted by a small London publishing house called Bloomsbury. Joanne was overjoyed, but the money did not start coming immediately. Her agent advised her to find work, and Rowling worked as a French teacher during 1996. A year later, she managed to secure a Scottish Arts Council grant of £8000 so that she could continue writing.

1000 copies of *Harry Potter and the Philosopher's Stone* were produced during the first print run. Bloomsbury feared that the author's female name would prevent the book from appealing to boys and suggested that the book should be published under a gender-neutral name. Joanne Rowling decided to go with two initials before her last name, but the problem was that Jo did not have a middle name. She chose the name Kathleen, after her grandmother who had died when Jo was a child. J.K. Rowling appeared on the cover of *Harry Potter and the Philosopher's Stone* when it was published. In 1998, the year after the British publication of the book, Scholastic secured the rights for the US publication for an impressive $105,000 (US currency). It was released in America as *Harry Potter and the Sorcerer's Stone*.

Even before the American publication of Rowling's first book, she had completed and published the second, *Harry Potter and the Chamber of Secrets*, in the UK. This second book was released in the year 1999 in the US. The rest of the series followed in rapid succession, with *Harry Potter and the Prisoner of Azkaban* in 1999, *Harry Potter and the Goblet of Fire* in 2000, *Harry Potter and the Order of the Phoenix* in 2003, having taken the longest to write because it is the longest book, *Harry Potter and the Half-Blood Prince* in 2005, and the final novel, *Harry Potter and the Deathly Hallows*, in 2007.

> "Her books have been translated into 67 languages."

The smashing, unprecedented success of the books has made Rowling rich and famous in a few short years. Her books have been translated into 67 languages, and have been made into blockbuster films. The books are not only on the bestseller list individually, they have made Rowling the bestselling author in history. 400 million book copies, plus revenue from licensing and the other

> "They have made Rowling the bestselling author in history. 400 million book copies."

results of the book's success have made Jo a billionaire, the only author in history to achieve this status from writing.

Wealth Accumulation

The whole world knows by now that Joanne Rowling certainly did not start out moneyed. She was essentially penniless when she published her first book. The purchase of publishing rights in the US for the first book sent J.K. Rowling on her way to success. By the release of the fourth book, *Harry Potter and the Goblet of Fire*, sales of the book were breaking records in both the UK and the US. In the first day of its release, 372,775 copies were sold in the UK alone. The US sales during the first two days totalled an unprecedented three million copies.

> "She was essentially penniless when she published her first book."

By the time the sixth book was published, Rowling was an old hand at breaking records in literary sales. The release date of a new *Harry Potter* book was a global event, with bookstores staying open all night to allow the hordes of costumed children and adults alike to begin the buying frenzy at the stroke of midnight. Within the first 24 hours of the release of *Harry Potter and the Half-Blood Prince*, on 16th July 2005, nine million copies had sold.

> "Harry Potter and the Deathly Hallows accomplished this with 11 million copies sold on the first day in the US and UK."

Any sales record that Rowling could break would now be her own previous ones. The seventh and final book, *Harry Potter and the Deathly Hallows*, accomplished this with 11 million copies sold on the first day in the US and UK.

After the release of the first two books, Rowling struck a seven-figure deal for film rights with Warner Bros. In contrast to the common tales of movie studios who purchase film rights to a book and then completely remove the scripts from the control of the original authors, wreaking havoc on the plots and characters, Warner Bros. accepted a great deal of input from Rowling. She was able to put certain stipulations in the contract, such as the one that states that the films must be shot in Britain, with a British cast. She also asked and received an $18million donation from *Coca-Cola,* who won rights to product placement in the film. The donation went to reading charities. The first film was released in November 2001, adding to *Harry Potter*'s popularity, boosting book sales, and becoming a huge monetary success in its own right. The first six films grossed over $5 billion US. Within four years of finishing the novel while grabbing spare time in cafes, Rowling was a tremendous success.

Copies of the original Bloomsbury print run of 1000 books are estimated to be worth anywhere from £16,000 to £25,000. Even this low estimate is twice what Rowling received in grant money after the first book's publication, and over six times the amount of the advance she received for *Harry Potter and the Philosopher's Stone.*

Rowling first appeared on the list of *Forbes* billionaires in 2004. This meant that her fortune was estimated at one billion US dollars. At the time, Rowling insisted that she was not a billionaire, although she had plenty of money. In any case, she apparently had more money than anyone could easily count.

With wealth came many benefits, and a few problems. In 2009, the estate of a deceased author brought a plagiarism suit against Rowling, seeking £500 million in damages, almost the whole of Rowling's fortune. The very short booklet of *Willy the Wizard,* it was claimed, had been copied by Rowling and used for *Harry Potter.* She has since been sued by others. Her fame makes her a target for those who would like to get their hands on a piece of her fortune.

Lawsuits notwithstanding, she has maintained her billionaire status since first appearing on the *Forbes* list, with an estimated net worth hovering around the one billion dollar mark. The *Harry Potter* brand itself has a much greater estimated net worth of around £7 billion.

Rowling now owns five luxurious homes in England and Scotland.

Her riches will increase with the opening of the anticipated theme park in Universal Studios, Orlando, Florida, USA. At the age of 44 (2010), Rowling has seen all of the highs and lows of struggle and success. She is set for life, but plans to continue writing.

Rowling worked steadily, with a few necessary interruptions, on her books until the series was completed. On the day after Christmas, in 2001, Rowling married her second husband, Neil Michael Murray, an anaesthetist. A little over a year later, on 24th March 2003, the couple had their first child. David Gordon Rowling Murray was his name and Rowling took a short maternity leave from writing upon his birth. A second baby, Mackenzie Jean Rowling Murray, was born on 23rd January 2005.

> "She is the wealthiest author on earth."

Each sale and each book sold more and more copies, and are as loved as the first. She long had a series in mind, so she did not fall prey to trying to tack extra stories onto what really should have stood on its own.

She was recently listed as number 937 on *Forbes'* list of "The World's Billionaires". She is the wealthiest author on earth. She was able to build her fortune, first by creating the immensely popular characters, but afterward, by maintaining her hardworking practices and high personal standards. It might have been tempting to take things easy and rest on the success of the early books, but Rowling continued hard and steady work. It is rare that sequels, particularly in films, are as good or as popular as the originals, but Rowling's pen has produced magic from first to last.

Achievements and Foundations

Most of the world, extending outside the English-speaking world, is in some way aware of Rowling's achievements. She is the highest-grossing author of all time. Four of the books, upon their release, set records for the fastest-selling books in history, each of the latter three breaking the record of the previous one. Even the films based on the books have set records. The Harry Potter films comprise the highest grossing film series of all time.

> "Four of the books, upon their release, set records for the fastest-selling books in history."

Rowling has received many honours and accolades for her work. The books are so popular that they are credited with having a large social impact. Rowling's characters have sparked such an interest in children that many people believe that the books have revived an interest in literature that was waning with the advent of the computer age. It was certainly unprecedented to see children coming out in large crowds, clamouring for books, and talking their parents into letting them stay up late at night. One might not pay much attention to such activity at the release of a movie, or even a video game, but that excitement surrounding stacks of hardcover books was an encouraging sight for many onlookers.

Aside from the intrinsic benefits of her work on literacy, Rowling has developed or contributed to many charitable projects. She established her Volant Charitable Trust in the year 2000. One purpose of the fund is to relieve poverty. The organisation also supports the causes of children's aid, multiple sclerosis research and single-parent families. The trust, in part, states that aside from multiple sclerosis research, the funds are to go toward

"Charities and projects, whether national or community-based, at home or abroad, that alleviate social deprivation, with a particular emphasis on women's and children's issues."

Furthermore, Rowling is president of One Parent Families, having begun in 2000 as its ambassador. Since she is now the world's most famous (former) struggling single mother, she was a natural choice for the position. She collaborated with her friend Sarah Brown on a book of stories to benefit the charity.

She wrote two booklets in aid of Comic Relief in 2001. The small booklets purport to be copies of Hogwarts library books and proceeds go to the charity's fund to fight poverty. The books have raised nearly £16 million.

Rowling, along with MEP Emma Nicholson, founded the Children's High Level Group. The organisation is now called Lumos. The charity aims to provide aid to children in desperate situations.

The death of Rowling's mother from multiple sclerosis has inspired Rowling to donate money for research and treatment of the disease. Her donations, in part, allowed for the establishment of the Centre for Regenerative Medicine to be built at Edinburgh University.

A large number of other causes have also received support and donations from Rowling. She contributed a short piece of writing to be auctioned by Waterstones booksellers in aid of Dyslexia Action and PEN.

When Madeleine McCann, a young British girl, went missing in Portugal, Rowling donated almost half a million US dollars to the reward fund. She, along with some other very big names, such as Nelson Mandela and Al Gore, helped to write an introduction to published speeches by Gordon Brown. Proceeds from this work were donated to the Jennifer Brown Research Laboratory.

Rowling read at Radio City Music Hall, in the company of bestsellers John Irving and Stephen King, in 2006. The proceeds from this event went to the Haven Foundation. This charity helps artists who cannot work and do not have health insurance. Part of the profits were also donated to Doctors Without Borders.

Accolades have rained down on Joanne Rowling since she became successful. She now has many honorary degrees. These honours came from Napier University, the University of Edinburgh, St. Andrews University, and the University of Aberdeen. She also received an honorary degree from Harvard University after speaking at their commencement ceremony.

Rowling is even the recipient of the Legion d'honneur. She was accorded this honour in 2009.

The *Harry Potter* books began receiving honours not long after the publication of the very first book, which received the Nestle Smarties Book Prize in 1997, five months after its publication. Early the next year, the book won the coveted British Book Award for Children's Book of the Year. It also later won the Children's Book Award.

Rowling's second and third novels also won the Nestle Smarties Book Prize. Rowling was the first person to win this prize three consecutive times. She afterward withdrew her books from further consideration for the prize, allowing other authors to gain more attention.

In 2000, the Whitbread Children's Book of the Year Award went to Rowling for *Harry Potter and the Prisoner of Azkaban*. Also in 2000, after publishing *Harry Potter and the Goblet of Fire,* the fourth novel, Rowling was named author of the year at the 2000 British Book Awards.

Book six, *Harry Potter and the Half-Blood Prince,* was the British Book Awards' Book of the Year for 2006.

Recognition, honours and praise for the author have come thick and fast since she was first published. She has accepted many degrees, prizes and other honours. Rowling has also made sure to put effort, time and money into charitable projects. She has said, "I think you have a moral responsibility when you've been given far more than you need, to do wise things with it and give intelligently."

Joanne (J.K.) Rowling's Tips for Success

Many of the stories that we have heard outline people who have made it big, or were clearly on the road to success, starting at a very young age. Such is not quite the case with Joanne Rowling. Privately, she did know that she wanted to be a writer and began working at the age of six. This is very young indeed, comparable to the first noticeable activity of Richard Branson or Warren Buffett. However, she was not able to be successful very early in life. Becoming a successful writer is a difficult and uncertain game, like other careers in arts and entertainment fields.

Rowling needed to work other jobs, and her life went down other paths, before success came to her. She had actually reached the toughest point in her life just before her so-called instant success, and she did not succeed until her 30th year. However, she had been working hard at her passion her whole life. When the rewards finally came, they came on a huge scale, and Rowling was able to enjoy the fruits of her labour.

Her example certainly reveals that persistence and hard work pay off in the end. Writing is extremely difficult, gruelling work. Authors are driven to despair time and again over major works, and when writing a novel, especially, there is no reasonable chance of earning large rewards. So, self-motivation is crucial in Rowling's field, which goes hand in hand with persistence.

Rowling has stated:

- "You have to resign yourself to wasting lots of trees before you write anything really good. That's just how it is."

  The principle that underlies this statement applies to far more than just writing, or even creative fields. It can be applied to any type of ambition. The idea is that one must set out to learn, practice and make mistakes, and to keep going until one becomes skilful at the job. Many people think of a talent like Rowling's as an inborn gift that people either have or don't have. On the contrary, Rowling had been practicing her craft for over two decades before she produced *Harry Potter*. The perseverance here is obvious.

- "Destiny is a name often given in retrospect to choices that had dramatic consequences." Looking in at a successful person's story from the outside, it is tempting to see everything as the result of some urge, talent, or nudge from fate. However, successful people, just like anyone, have made decisions their whole lives. Just a few of these decisions end up really changing things for them. What they leave behind are many choices which either did not work out, or only produced small results. The point is that they keep trying until they do find something that pays off.

- It is perhaps not surprising that many people ask Rowling for the secret formula to her success. She is reluctant to answer this question, saying, "I've never analysed it that way and I think it would be dangerous for me to start analysing it or thinking that way. I don't want it to stop being fun, and – number two – I'm not sure I know. After all," she adds, "the correct people to ask are the readers."

While Rowling does not come out and say so, by reading between the lines we can actually see a formula for her success in this statement. "I don't want it to stop being fun...." She says. We can infer from this a basic idea that leads people to their goals, and that is the idea of pursuing one's passion, whatever one is interested in and finds joy or satisfaction in.

- Rowling was asked if she was surprised about the fact that she has an adult audience, in addition to the obvious market for children. She is not. She has said, "When I write the books, I really do write them for me. Very often I get asked, 'Who do you have in mind when you write? Is it your daughter or is it the children you've met?' No. It's for me. Just for me. I'm very selfish—I write for me."

> "Create what you want to see in the world."

This shows the fact that one really cannot do good work if it is merely in order to please other people. The notion that you need to create things for yourself contains echoes of advice from Richard Branson: create what you want to see in the world. You cannot read anyone else's mind, and only you know the ins and outs of what you want to create and why.

- She also says that, "Anything's possible if you've got enough nerve." Successful people have the courage of their convictions. They also set about achieving their goals, without being stopped by obstacles. These obstacles might be time, money, motivation, or other people. There are always doors that need to be opened, and this cannot be

> "Successful people have the courage of their convictions."

done without risking rejection and even embarrassment. However, success is made by simply trying and keeping at it until the doors open. This does take nerve.

Summary

Rowling's story is one of working through difficulties and challenges and not stopping despite discouragement and outside pressures. As far as the public could see, she did not start early. Harry Potter may have come to the attention of the public as he came to Joanne Rowling, fully formed and developed, ready to spring to life.

However, for the author of bestsellers, if not for the public, that moment of inspiration was not magic. It came only after years of patient effort, practice and hard work. Rowling wrote two other novels before she wrote the Harry Potter books. She did not even attempt to publish them. She was simply honing her skills, working hard at the things that she loved to do.

The central lesson to be learned from Rowling's story is one of perseverance. In Rowling's case, success did not come in bits and pieces, keeping pace with the effort that was put forth over the years. Her story shows the true hard work that must precede success, whether it comes slowly or suddenly.

Larry Page

"Fear of failure should not stop anyone."

MILLIONAIRES
& BILLIONAIRES

SECRETS
REVEALED!

Brief Overview

Larry Page

Born: 26th March, 1973, in Lansing, Michigan, USA

Business: Google Inc.

Industry: Information Technology

Income: $17.5 billion

Lives: California, USA

Family: Wife, Lucinda Southworth

Charities: Google.org

Status: Billionaire

Larry Page

Profile

Larry page is one of the richest and most successful men in the world, and yet many people have never even heard of him. One name that everyone does recognise, however, is Google. Page, along with his partner, Sergey Brin, founded the search engine, and head Google, Inc.

He was recently among the top 25 wealthiest people in the world. And this is his fortune—his partner is tied with him, because they are worth the same, as co-founders of the business. The explosive growth of Google, Inc. has so transformed the way we do things that it is hard to imagine that it was created little over a decade ago.

> "...recently among the top 25 wealthiest people in the world."

Page is a single-minded man. That's no surprise, since it would take such laser focus to earn the fortune that he has.

Larry Page has always played with computers. At the time of this writing, Page is still only in his mid-30s. Yet, he has created a program that has become a household name and is even used as a verb (as in, "I don't know, I'll Google it"), and he has made a mind-boggling fortune.

His example is one of focused purpose, the importance of collaboration and putting moral thinking into one's work. He built a business that is actually based on sending his customers elsewhere. This novel approach revolutionised modern culture and a modern way of making profits.

Background

Lawrence Edward Page was born on 26 March, 1973, in Lansing, Michigan, USA. Larry Page had an unusual beginning. His parents were both professors in the field of computing. Dr. Carl Victor Page, Larry's father, taught at Michigan State University as a professor of computer science and artificial intelligence. Gloria Page, Larry's mother, taught computer programming. This might not be remarkable now, but in the early 1970s, computers were a new science, not even grasped by the general public. Larry Page's future might have been set before he was born.

The house where Larry grew up was full of early computers and copies of *Popular Science* magazines. This strange environment allowed Larry to begin tinkering with computers when he was a child, which is exactly what he did.

Page's educational foundation began at Okemos Montessori School in Michigan. He says that he was the "first kid in my elementary school to turn in an assignment from a word processor" since he was already familiar with computers at home. Even at this age, he loved to take apart his parents' computers to find out how they worked. He has said that, "From a very early age, I also realised I wanted to invent things. So I became really interested in technology and business. So probably from when I was 12 I knew I was going to start a company eventually."

He later attended East Lansing High School. After graduating in 1991, he attended the University of Michigan. He graduated from here with a BS in computer engineering. He graduated with honours and moved on to graduate studies at Stanford University in Palo Alto, California, in computer science.

While at Stanford, Larry met Sergey Brin in 1995. Brin had been born in Moscow, Russia, immigrating to the states while still a child. Brin, also a computer science student, was attending Stanford on a National Science Foundation fellowship. The two did not really take to one another at first, each considering the other to be "obnoxious". However, they soon began collaborating on projects, due to their mutual interests and mutual clear intelligence.

Page had begun working on a project related to the World Wide Web, encouraged by a professor. Page was looking at the ways in which web pages were linked to one another. At first, Page worked on a way to find out how many pages on the Web were linked to any other page. Search engines at that time could only determine how many times any particular word appeared on a certain page. Therefore, web searches produced results simply based on particular words and often returned huge lists of irrelevant searches.

Page was interested in ranking pages, or websites, based not purely on the frequency of a word, but also on the number of links that led from a site to any given other site. His friend Sergey Brin had expertise in data mining, having already written over a dozen papers on the subject.

Brin was interested because of the project's complexity. At that time, there were an estimated 10 million pages on the Web, any of which could potentially be linked to any other. The two went to work on the complex project, and the result was two papers. The second paper, with the mouthful of a title, "The Anatomy of a Large-Scale Hypertextual Web Search Engine", made a splash in tech circles. Soon after they wrote it, the paper had been downloaded more frequently than almost any other scientific document on the Internet.

They had developed their new search engine, describing it in that paper. The program was then called "BackRub", and it was run on the motley collection of personal computers in Page's dormitory room.

Very quickly, the two boys realised that they were onto something. They renamed the page, and the google.com domain name was registered in 1997. The name was chosen as a derivation of the word "googol", which is the name of an enormous number that consists of a one followed by 100 zeros. They chose the name to represent the enormous amounts of data that would be coordinated by their search engine.

> "The name was chosen as a derivation of the word "googol", which is the name of an enormous number that consists of a one followed by 100 zeros."

By that time, Page had completed his Master's degree in computer science. He and Brin decided to take a leave of absence from their PhD. Program in order to work on their new business. Google was incorporated in 1998 and they moved out of the dormitory room into their new digs—a friend's garage. They were now in Menlo Park, California. Larry Page was the CEO of the company, and Sergey Brin was its president. Their mission statement read that Google's aim was "to organise the world's information and make it universally accessible and useful."

> "It was difficult to finance the growth of the company... we had to use all of our credit cards and our friends' credit cards and our parents' credit cards."

Google took off right away. Page and Brin had a hard time keeping up with their own company, which was growing at astounding rates of up to 205% each *month*. For one thing, they moved frequently, since they quickly outgrew every facility that they moved into. They eventually settled on a large campus in Mountain View, California. For another, it was difficult to finance the growth of the company. Page says that, "We had to use all of our credit cards and our friends' credit cards and our parents' credit cards." Eventually, they received enough private investments to fund the growing company, with the funds coming through Stanford.

In 2001, Page and Brin had recruited a new Chief Executive Officer. Eric Schmidt left his position with Novell to serve at Google. The restructuring left Larry Page free to assume the new role of President for Products and Sergey Brin took the title of President for Technology. The company was still seeing its astronomical growth, which seemed to have no end. Google had set up one of the most unusual and innovative working environments in the world and attracted some of the best brains in the field.

> "...became multi-billionaires almost immediately."

The company made its public offering in 2004 and entered the market in the values of billions. Not only Larry Page and Brin, but other employees of the young company, became multibillionaires almost immediately. Larry Page (and Sergey Brin) was 27 years old. Google continued on its pattern of amazing growth. Google made acquisitions of other sites to increase the engines' value. They acquired power player YouTube in 2006.

> "Larry Page is now one of the wealthiest men on earth, appearing at number 24 on the Forbes' list of the World's Richest People in 2010."

A 2007 issue of *Fortune* magazine called Google the world's best company to work for. With Page and Brin at the helm, Google continues to innovate and to grow in value. Larry Page is now one of the wealthiest men on earth, appearing at number 24 on the *Forbes* 'list of the World's Richest People in 2010.

Wealth Accumulation

Larry Page is in an unusual position among the success stories that we have been exploring. He is the only one to have made his fortune with a full partner, Sergey Brin, instead of single-handedly creating a fortune. They have split everything, building the company so closely together that the two still share an office. Their fortune has been evenly divided, too. So, the already massively impressive fortune of Larry Page can actually be doubled when considering the founders and presidents of Google.

> "The two presidents and the CEO of Google each collect an annual pay check of exactly one US dollar."

The great explosion of growth and wealth is even more impressive when we consider an unusual decision made by Page and Brin, with their CEO, Eric Schmidt, following suit. After the company went public in 2004, making the founders billionaires, they gave up their salaries. The two presidents and the CEO of Google each collect an annual pay check of exactly one US dollar. They have also refused company bonuses. Their income, therefore, is strictly the profits from company stock, which ties the income of the men directly to Google's performance on the market.

This income is, of course, still almost unimaginable. After Google went public in 2004, Page first made the *Forbes* list of the World's Richest People. He was number 552 on this list, and number 43 on The Forbes 400, which ranks the Richest in America. His worth that year, at the age of 31, was estimated at $4 billion.

By the following year, Page's fortune had moved him up to 55th on the World's Richest People list. He was then worth an estimated $12.8 billion. In 2007, his fortune had grown to $18.5 billion, putting Page at number 26 on the list of the World's Richest People.

By 2008, many people had lost money, including Page. He had slipped to number 33 in the world. Although his net worth had increased by one million dollars in the preceding year, to $18.6 billion, the growth of Google slowed during the economic downturn.

By the next year, Page was back up to number 26. Although his net worth had fallen to $12 billion, wealth had generally fallen across the board, and Google was performing better than many businesses.

"He was estimated to be worth $17.5 billion."

At last count, Larry Page was at number 24 in the world, his net worth having risen almost back to its previous high point. He was estimated to be worth $17.5 billion.

Page, along with Brin, produced his tremendous success with a single ingenious idea. From his days playing with the computers that were lying around his parents' house, he had developed an early interest in technology. When he began working on his dissertation at Stanford, he simply had a problem to solve. What is the best way to search for pages on the internet, considering the way they are linked? Finding the solution to that problem solved some problems for everyone who used the internet. It made Larry Page, and his friend and business partner Sergey Brin, wealthy at a very young age. Page and Brin are still under 40 years old, and rank among the wealthiest men on the planet.

Achievements and Foundations

Larry Page has made his mark on the world quickly and decisively. In a remarkably short time, he and Brin have turned a school project into one of the cornerstones of the internet. Is there anyone who uses a computer who does not search with Google at least part of the time?

Google has received many awards for technical achievement. The "Webby Awards" have been bestowed on Google in many different categories. PC Magazine named Google among its 1998 Top 100 Web Sites and Search engines. This was only a year after the site was launched, and the year in which the Google domain name was registered. Google was a breakthrough right from the beginning. The following year, PC Magazine chose Google to receive its Technical Excellence Award for Innovation in Web Application and Development.

Now that Page has been so successful in the worlds of technology and business, he has also made it a point to concentrate on alternative ways of improving the world around him.

Google tries many creative projects to improve their sustainability at The Googleplex, as the campus is known.

Larry Page has been interested in sustainable technology for almost as long as he has been interested in computers. Even while Page was attending the University of Michigan for his undergraduate studies, he was a member of the solar car team, racing innovative cars that are designed with solar power.

Now that Page has the money to invest in causes, he has invested in alternative energy companies. One of these was Tesla Motors. This company created the Tesla Roadster, an electric vehicle. The car can run for 350 km on a battery charge. Google has a philanthropic division, Google.org, which helps to advance alternative energy.

Page has been recognised with awards and accolades for his success. Both Page and Sergey Brin received honorary Master's of Business Administration degrees from IE Business School, which stated that the degree was "for embodying the entrepreneurial spirit and lending momentum to the creation of new businesses."

In 2004, the year Google went public, they received an engineering award, the Marconi Foundation Prize. They were also elected fellows of the Marconi Foundation at Columbia University.

Page was named a Global Leader for Tomorrow by the World Economic Forum. He received an honorary doctorate degree from the University of Michigan in 2009, speaking at the commencement ceremonies. That same year, Page and Brin appeared at number 5 on *Forbes'* list of The World's Most Powerful People.

Page is a man who achieved more by his 20s than many people do over a lifetime. He has the honours to prove it.

Larry Page's Tips for Success

Larry Page shot to dizzying heights like a rocket. There is an element of luck in his story. Not everyone was born to parents who happened to be experts in a new technology that was ready to take off in the popular commercial sector. But even with that, Larry Page made the absolute most of every opportunity. He did extremely well in school. So well, in fact, that one of his projects at university was the project that would launch his ultra-successful business.

Once he realised what he had, he simply ran with it. He worked extremely hard to allow the company to keep up with customer demand. The company made Page a billionaire in his late 20s.

Page notes that, while other companies are trying to outdo the competition, their company is in the business of sending users elsewhere.

- "We built a business on the opposite message. We want you to come to Google and quickly find what you want. Then we're happy to send you to the other sites. In fact, that's the point."

  > "We built a business on the opposite message."

Instead of trying to gather information and keep users at Google, they built a search engine that would allow users to find what they were looking for, and quickly go elsewhere. This filled a need that is obvious now that Google is so successful. Part of the lesson here is to think in new and creative ways. Question even the most basic tenets about how to do business. If you can find a way to serve many people in a new way, you have a formula for success on your hands.

  > "...things do change, and if your business is static, you're likely to have issues."

- "Many leaders of big organisations don't believe that change is possible. But if you look at history, things do change, and if your business is static, you're likely to have issues."

The pace of living and doing business is changing faster now than ever before. The rapid pace of change is actually due, in part, to Larry Page, among others. This is a lesson about adaptability. If you can see the next big thing on the horizon, and adapt to it, you can ride the wave to prosperity.

- Google has a simple company mantra; "Don't be evil." The leaders of Google maintain their integrity and moral thinking, and make it part of their corporate culture. Page says, "Our users trust Google's objectivity and no short-term gain could ever justify breaching that trust." This determination to do things well and with principle has led to their gaining the trust of vast numbers of people.

- Page's company places a premium on true excellence. "Always deliver more than expected. Google does not accept being the best as an endpoint, but a starting point." This point about standards is a major insight. Don't just do things, do them well. Do them better than anyone else. And then surpass your own mark. With that kind of mindset, it would be impossible not to succeed, and one can see why Google is the brand that it is.

  > **"Always deliver more than expected."**

- Page doesn't simply think in terms of providing a quality service to make Google the best search engine. He thinks big, and puts that thinking into his business. In everything Page and Google do, he has an eye toward improving the world. He set up his company that way, he makes sure that his employees are empowered to work in that way, and he wants to offer users the tools to work that way, too. He says "Talented people are attracted to Google because we empower them to change the world."

  > **"Talented people are attracted to Google because we empower them to change the world."**

- Page also notes that fear of failure should not stop anyone. "My experience is that when people are trying to do ambitious things, they're all worried about failing when they start. But all sorts of interesting things spin out that are of huge economic value. Also, in these kinds of projects, you get to work with the best people and have a very interesting time. They're not really taking a risk, but they feel like they are."

- Page places emphasis on giving users everything they want, and letting his employees take control and be unfettered when they are looking for solutions. Google does not have a large administrative structure to bog things down. Page says simply, "We don't have as many managers as we should, but we would rather have too few than too many."

> "Fear of failure should not stop anyone."

- Finally, Page thinks in simple terms about providing for the needs of his customer base. "Serving our end users is at the heart of what we do and remains our number one priority."

Google is the best at what it does. It allows anyone, from anywhere, to find any information, at any time. This extraordinary achievement is what made Larry Page a success.

Summary

Larry Page is one of the richest men on earth. In the company of the rest of the world's wealth, he is a very young player. He started working with computers at a very young age and, in some ways, he did little else through his whole life. He has also always spent time on his other big interest, sustainable technology.

This single vision enabled Page to start the project that would change his life, and the world. He had succeeded so well in school that he was able to attend one of the best institutions of learning in the world. This environment allowed him the opportunity and encouragement to pursue his complex project.

Page is unusual in his emphasis on collaboration. Brin has been with him from the beginning. The two built Google into what it is today and they continue to bring a spirit of collaboration to their corporate culture. All of their employees benefit from the ability to work with anyone.

Finally, Page and Brin are both outstanding among businessmen, and even among most people, for their uncompromising conviction. They make their corporate environment as sustainable as possible. They both refuse to give an inch when it comes to the integrity of Google, as a company and as an online service. That has spelled success on a huge scale for Larry Page.

Authors' Final Word

We have now heard nine extraordinary stories. What can we learn about wealth and success from the renegade Richard Branson, the powerful Bill Clinton, the phenomenal Oprah Winfrey, the questioning Pierre Omidyar, the fiercely hard-driving genius Bill Gates, the simple and steady Warren Buffett, the charismatic Tony Blair, the magically creative Joanne "J.K." Rowling and the boy wonder Larry Page?

We can distill these stories down into three main concepts.

The first is purpose. All of the people that have been outlined have started with, and maintained, a crystal-clear vision. No matter what that vision was, they begin with an idea of what they wanted to do with their lives, and they kept that vision, at the base of everything, throughout their lives and careers.

The second concept is passion. The people we have heard about don't simply have a purpose—they believe in that purpose with their whole hearts and minds. They carry a core of conviction that keeps them performing at their own, near-impossible, standards. No matter what obstacles they face, they believe that what they are trying to accomplish is the most important thing they could be doing.

The third and last concept is what allows the first two to be translated into action. Hard work—pure sweat, stamina and discipline, created all of these success stories. They work for work and they sometimes work for fun. But, above all, they work to achieve their purpose and to carry out their passion.

These principles might seem fairly obvious and easy to grasp. But, if we compare our success stories to an average life, they are the qualities that stand out most strongly. The fact is that most people do not carry through, every day, with a single-minded purpose and an eye on the goal.

Now, the strategies for creating wealth and success have been revealed. Go ahead and implement these strategies. You, too, can become a success story.

About the Authors

Darren Stephens

Entrepreneur, Author, Speaker and Business Consultant

Darren is a self-made multimillionaire and is a seasoned business executive, entrepreneur, growth strategist, bestselling author and consultant.

Darren was the founder and International Chairman of Mars Venus Coaching, one of the world's most respected and leading brands, and is now the Managing Director of global businesses such as Global Media Group and Successful Growth Strategies.

He is also a board member and International Franchise Director of the world's No# 1 eBay education company, Bidding Buzz Global Limited, with offices in 11 countries, including Australia, Rome, Paris, Singapore, Hong Kong, UK and North America.

He's recognised as an expert in the field of business development, sales and marketing, executive mentoring, franchising, international publishing, self-development and accelerated psychological transformation.

He is the author of 7 best-selling books such as "Top Franchise CEO's Secrets Revealed", "The 10 Day Turnaround, "The Success Principles" and "Our Internet Secrets," just to name a few. He was also the marketing genius behind developing the expansion of the Mars Venus brand, now in 150 countries and the books of which have been translated into 54 languages and have generated over a billion dollars in sales.

For more than 20 years, Darren has taught internationally, speaking to and motivating thousands of people in over 27 countries on how to create business, personal and financial success.

Darren's appearances on many television programs, and his articles published in newspapers and magazines nationally and internationally, has made him a sought-after speaker and consultant on the international stage.

Darren has also lectured at University on business management, marketing and psychological transformation and he is a certified Hypnotist, Neuro-Linguistic Programming (NLP) trainer and is qualified in Design Human Engineering and Time Line Therapy.

He is a fellow diplomat of the American Board of Hypnotherapy and a member of the International Franchise Association, Franchise Council of Australia National Speakers Association and is the founder of the prestigious Entrepreneurs Business School.

He lives in Melbourne, Australia, with his wife, Jackie, and their 7 children.

www.DarrenJStephens.com

Spike Humer

Spike Humer is a highly successful entrepreneur, consultant and deal-maker with more than twenty-five years of real world, hands-on experience leading both public and private companies throughout North America. As an international speaker, growth strategist and performance expert he changes businesses and lives worldwide. In 2003, Spike founded Spike Humer International and currently serves as CEO.

Spike Humer International, a consulting and training firm, specialises in all aspects of business mentoring, individual and organisational performance enhancement, strategy setting and tactical execution. Specific applications include strategic planning, management assessment and leadership training, joint venture development, marketing, sales training and small business turnarounds.

Spike has served as the COO and Chief Consultant for The Abraham Group and Jay Abraham, who is considered to be one of the world's preeminent marketing consultants and business strategists. Oftentimes co-presenting and co-consulting with Jay Abraham, Spike Humer has been a major collaborator on The Abraham Group's seminars, workshops, mentoring programs and private client consultations throughout Asia, Australia and North America. Spike has also worked with Jay Abraham and The Abraham Group as its top deal-maker and joint venture strategist.

Jay Abraham said, "Spike is probably the finest business performance enhancement specialist" he has ever met and, "An utter master at finding the underperforming leveraging spots that are keeping your business from soaring."

Spike has coached, counseled, consulted and taught individuals and businesses in over twenty-three countries. He has appeared on the same speaking programs as such notable speakers and authors as Brian Tracy, Chet Holmes, Mark Victor Hansen, T. Harv Eker, Stephen M.R. Covey, Seth Godin, John Assaraf, Brendon Burchard, Stephen Pierce, Rich Schefren and many other industry thought-leaders.

Throughout his career he has designed, led and implemented highly successful turnaround and organisational restructurings for small to midsized organisations. His advice, guidance and leadership have reinvigorated the image, reputation and performance of companies and corporations using a "strategy of significance" and by creating a top-to-bottom culture of service, authenticity and accountability.

Widely regarded as a leading expert on business and personal change, Spike is the co-author of the book "The 10 Day Turnaround for Business" and the developer of "The 10 Day Turnaround for Life" seminar and book series.

www.SpikeHumer.com

Recommended Success Resources

How To Save Time & Achieve Extraordinary Results …In Less Than 1 Day

What if you could achieve extraordinary results and experience the total satisfaction of knowing just how far you've progressed toward your goals and objectives every step along the way? Imagine the power of knowing you are doing the right things, in the right order, and at the right time!!

The 10 Day Turnaround Priority Management System is a breakthrough in both business and life management that will show you how to align your activities and your laser your focus instead of just simply trying to organize your time, giving you the freedom and peace of mind to pursue your passions.

The 10 Day Turnaround Priority Management System helps you:

- Set priorities using the powerful 80/20 Principle of getting the most from the least

- Break through uncertainty and hesitation to take decisive action now

- Align your actions with your goals and turn them into success and profit

- Set clear direction and plot a course for a more fulfilling role and life

- Create immediate "wins" as well as lasting success

- Regain the certainty that you are in control of your business and life

- Immediately move from an activity orientation to a results focus

- Dramatically increase your level of productivity

- Replace your To-Do list with an effective plan that maximizes your time and guarantees you accomplish key tasks

- Create a powerful sense of purpose, drive and fulfillment every day

- Enhance your project management systems to turn ideas into reality

- Track your progress, learn from past experiences and celebrate your success.

The unique software has been developed from years of real-world success to show you how to gain control over your present and to design the future you desire.

"How To Turn The "Profit Tap" On FULL STREAM & Plug The Leaking Holes In Your Business 10 Days or Less"

Why it's **CRITICAL & URGENT** to implement a "Turnaround" before it's too late...

It could simply be that, you believe your business is not living up to its true potential. It could also be that you want to understand clearly where your business is at that moment, where you want it to be in the future so that a concise plan of action can be developed to get it there.

Maybe you want to build you business up so you can sell out for a BIG PAY DAY - or maybe you want to take advantage of changes in the marketplace or of a new opportunity, or on completion of your own business-building practice.

The reasons why a business embarks on a turnaround plan are many and varied. However, it would probably be fair to say that during times of turmoil hardship, or a tough economy - **for the vast majority of businesses, embarking on a turnaround plan is most likely so that it can survive.** That is why we look at an extremely short time frame in which to achieve this. It should take you no longer than ten days to come up with a powerfully clear, concise, and actionable plan to transform the business.

To find out more about our Home Study DVD program simply visit our website.

The Amazing Web Site Copy Writing Software That Spits Out 100 Profit Pulling Headlines In Just 17 Seconds!

Headline Creator Pro is an amazing piece of software that gives you power to instantly create winning headlines. You'll never be stuck for a headline with Headline Creator Pro, the preferred copy writing software. You'll have 100 headlines to choose from in just 17 seconds – how long would you spend doing that by hand? How long do you spend waiting on your content writer to create excellent headlines, that really work? Or even make you money ?

Headline creator Pro provides you headlines with proven results to optimise response rate. Regardless of your business size, its time to move up to the pros.

Joint Venture Deals That Can Make You Millions!

Spike & Darren have developed something of a world famous skill and reputation at understanding how to structure, program and profit-massively by engineering joint ventures, strategic alliances and endorsement deals.

Without exaggerating, it represents the biggest, fastest, most lucrative revenue source, profit centre or income stream YOU could ever create, control and reap financial rewards from.

You'll be able to gain control of products, services, assets, profit centres, brands, entities, markets --- for zero capital outlay on your part. In fact, We plan on teaching you 48 separate ways you can prosper from doing J.V. deals···for yourself, for others, or even for us!

Inside You'll Discover:

- Getting the ancillary rights to prominent brands -- on a pure, performance-based payment basis.

- Eight strategic steps to make any JV deal a huge moneymaker!

- How to instantly identify every business's hidden JV possibilities.

- Seven steps to expand your own financial growth possibilities as a JV deal maker.

- Finding powerful, profitable JV partners to align with who'll do all the work for you.

- How to profit massively from competitive companies weaknesses and gaps.

- You'll learn exactly how to make the successful JV deal happen.

- At the very end, I'll give you a 20-step, "mind-expanding," exercise to rapidly propel your deal making career into the financial stratosphere.

- You'll learn seven different ways to get equity/ownership through no-cost JV deals

- You'll learn how to gain"no cost" access to other people's core competencies, skills and expertise

How To Write A Book Special Home Study Program: for Professionals and Non Professionals…

World Publishing Expert & International Bestselling Author Darren Stephens Reveals a Complete, No-Holds-Barred Success System for Getting Your Book to Market.

You will Discover:

- How to have a Best Seller even if you failed English at school.

- How to build a Multi Million dollar business as an Author.

- 21 Simple ways to get free publicity for your new book

- How to turn your hard copy book into an ebook & downloadable audio so you can sell it online for passive income

- How to make $195,000 in just 2 weeks using our book model

- How to make sure you're making the right choice about whether to go with a publisher or self–publish (don't underestimate the importance of this vital decision!)

- The leveraged business model used by major authors to build a multi-million dollar empire around their book.

- Techniques for writing quickly, easily and well even if you're hopeless with grammar and spelling!

- Marketing systems including online and offline marketing strategies

- How to get Major celebrities to endorse your book

- Finding powerful, profitable JV partners to align with who'll do all the work for you.

- How to profit massively from competitive companies weaknesses and gaps.

Bringing Essential Knowledge & Book Summaries to High Achievers

The International Achievement Institute is an Global Educational company designed to promote and present world class programs and provide transformative business and personal knowledge to individuals.

To Find out more about the Institutes educational materials & programs like these :

1. Entrepreneurs Business School

2. Entrepreneurs Board Room

3. The 10 Day Turnaround workshops

4. Accelerate Performance Technology Trainings

5. Essential Book Summaries

Change Your Life Today !!

Visit our Website at…
www.TheInternationalAchievementInstitute.com

"The real source of wealth and capital in this new era is not material things. It is the human mind, the human spirit, the human imagination and our ability to take massive action and our faith in the future."

Darren J Stephens